ALLENTOWN STATE HOSPITAL

IMAGES of America

On the Cover: This image is believed to be from the late 1950s to early 1960s. The car is a 1958 Ford Fairlane that most likely belonged to Dr. Howard T. Fiedler, superintendent of Allentown State Hospital from 1955 to 1972. The superintendent's living quarters are above the main entrance. (Courtesy of the Pennsylvania State Archives.)

IMAGES of America
ALLENTOWN STATE HOSPITAL

Steven Royer
Foreword by Gregory Smith

Copyright © 2020 by Steven Royer
ISBN 978-1-4671-0512-5

Published by Arcadia Publishing
Charleston, South Carolina

Printed in the United States of America

Library of Congress Control Number: 2019957033

For all general information, please contact Arcadia Publishing:
Telephone 843-853-2070
Fax 843-853-0044
E-mail sales@arcadiapublishing.com
For customer service and orders:
Toll-Free 1-888-313-2665

Visit us on the Internet at www.arcadiapublishing.com

This book is dedicated to all the former patients of the Allentown State Hospital and the thousands of staff who throughout the past century helped bring recovery and hope to the Lehigh Valley's most vulnerable citizens.

Contents

Foreword   6

Acknowledgments   7

Introduction   8

1. Building Pennsylvania's First Homeopathic State Hospital   11
2. The Epoch-Making Years   33
3. Farm Life and the Weaversville Colonies   47
4. Building for the Future   59
5. Turnover and Treatment   77
6. A New Era   91
7. PERT and the Road Ahead   101
8. Fighting for Tomorrow   115

Foreword

Allentown State Hospital (ASH) will most likely be gone by the time Steven Royer's work is published. The 200-acre campus has been cleared and made ready for the next phase of its development. When the heavy equipment has completed its work, I expect there will be little physical evidence of the 100-year history, both good and bad, at 1600 Hanover Avenue, which is why this book is so important.

Throughout its history, ASH was a community, providing care, treatment, and services to Pennsylvania's most vulnerable citizens. If you had a family member who lived in the Allentown area during the last century who needed extended treatment for a mental health condition, it is likely they had contact with the hospital.

The hospital's initial approach to care when it opened in 1912 was homeopathic treatment. In its final years, ASH embraced the recovery approach to psychiatric care and services, which served as a guide for the care they provided and the changes that would occur in its final years.

It was during these final years that ASH made its greatest and most lasting contribution to inpatient psychiatric and behavioral healthcare services. Through its positive approach to supporting people in crisis with its Psychiatric Emergency Response Teams (PERT), they were able to reduce and eventually eliminate the use of seclusion, and later mechanical restraint as a procedure in supporting a patient in crisis. The success of PERT, as evidenced in published research, led to a safer hospital and unexpected national and international attention.

Since then, the PERT approach has been adopted by many hospitals and systems of care worldwide and is now part of the World Health Organization's recently published QualityRights initiative. Coupled with its emphasis on recovery, ASH made a significant, positive difference in the lives of the people they served and became a worldwide model for the non-offensive care and treatment of people with a serious mental illness.

Finally, most of what ASH was able to achieve during its nearly 100-year existence is attributable to the diverse people who worked at the hospital and their constant commitment to quality care. The Lehigh Valley should be proud of the work they did. While the hospital has closed, many of the former staff continue to leave easy footprints for future generations of caregivers to follow.

—Gregory M. Smith, MS
Chief Executive Officer, Allentown State Hospital
1997–2009

Acknowledgments

Allentown State Hospital became a leader in mental health care thanks to dedicated staff and volunteers. These individuals committed their careers to providing the best patient care possible and deserve recognition for outstanding work. I would also like to applaud all who participated in and helped develop the Psychiatric Emergency Response Team (PERT). Your success continues to inspire other mental health facilities to reduce the use of seclusion and restraints.

On January 6, 2019, Brooke Kemler established a change.org petition against the demolition of Allentown State Hospital that is mentioned toward the end of this book. It climbed to over 6,400 signatures by the end of 2019, which helped to generate public interest in the hospital. Her dedication to seeing the history of Allentown State Hospital saved inspired me to start this project.

A tremendous thank-you is owed to Gregory Smith, CEO of ASH from 1997 to 2009. Smith served as a mentor to me throughout this process and helped me write chapter seven. His passion for the humane treatment of those suffering from mental illness is inspiring.

This book would not have been completed without the help of John McDevitt. His wealth of knowledge from 35 years of service at ASH and ability to remember the smallest of details was a saving grace throughout this entire process. I would also like to credit him for his efforts of documenting the history of the hospital before this project even started. Those efforts served as a foundation for this book.

I would like to extend a very special thank-you to Bill Jesse, Leslie Pirl-Roth, Cynthia Kromer, Colleen Kulhamer, Shawn McClure, Robert Lewis, the Jay family, and Theresa O'Dea. Pirl-Roth helped me network and provided articles on ASH from the museum at Wernersville State Hospital (WSH). She is by far one of the best librarians this world has ever seen and does an above-and-beyond job of maintaining WSH's museum. Kromer and Kulhamer provided me with extensive knowledge and stories of the hospital's grounds, which helped greatly. Jesse opened up his grandfather Harry Anderson's collection of artifacts and stories. McClure provided one of the few remaining invitations to the cornerstone laying ceremony, an amazing piece of history. Lewis contributed images from his extensive collection of asylum postcards.

I would also like to recognize authors who helped answer questions during the beginning of this project: J. Gregory Pirmann, Katherine Anderson, Phillip N. Thomas, and Rusty Tagliareni. These four do amazing work preserving the history of institutes similar to Allentown State Hospital, and some of their books can be found on www.arcadiapublishing.com.

One of my first pieces of ASH history came from the photo album of nurse Janice Painter, who worked and lived on the grounds of the hospital. A huge thank-you to her son Frank Reese and grandson Witt Reese for providing me with permission to use them.

Finally, a huge thank-you to Tyler Stump and the staff of the Pennsylvania State Archives. Their hard work in organizing and preserving the documents of the state hospital helped complete this book. All photographs credited to the Pennsylvania State Archives (excluding construction photos) come from Record Group 23, Records of the Department of Public Welfare; Office of Mental Health; Allentown State Hospital, Series 23.963 and 23.956. Construction images come from Record Group 9, Records of the General State Authority, Construction Photographs and Blueprints, 1932-1939, Series 1.

This book is the result of research conducted by the author and does not represent the opinions or views of the Pennsylvania Department of Human Services, OMHSAS, or Allentown State Hospital. Faces of patients have been blurred in some photographs to protect their privacy.

Introduction

The chief justice of colonial Pennsylvania's Supreme Court, William Allen, began laying out the plans for the city of Allentown (at the time called Northamptontown) toward the end of the colonial period in 1762. At this time, the concept of an institution to care strictly for the mentally ill was new. Throughout towns and cities there were instead almshouses, also known as poor houses. The Lehigh Valley was no exception, and from 1831 to the early 1840s, residents petitioned the county to build an almshouse. Eventually, the county obliged, and an almshouse was built in 1845.

Throughout the country, these public institutions generally became the "cure-all" solution for what society deemed unacceptable or impossible to manage. Halls would be lined with the mentally ill, prostitutes, elderly who no longer could afford rent, the blind or deaf, those infected with tuberculosis, and abandoned children. These places had no standards of sanitation or safety, and little to no medical care was provided. If an individual entered into an almshouse, disease or a rapidly diminishing mental state was almost guaranteed.

It was not until the mid-18th century when different ideas on how to treat those with mental illness began to emerge. The Pennsylvania Hospital, the first hospital in the United States, was founded by Benjamin Franklin and Dr. Thomas Bond in Philadelphia on May 11, 1751, and opened its doors in 1753. Treatment for all types of patients was provided here, including those who suffered from mental illness. Bloodletting, a procedure based on the belief that draining blood from the body would cure an illness, was the preferred treatment of Dr. Rush, who worked at the hospital and was one of the founders of American psychiatry. This treatment seemed to work, in that it created a calmer patient, the result of severe weakness caused by a large amount of blood loss.

Almshouses continued to be overcrowded in Pennsylvania, along with the rest of the country. A new solution on how to house and treat the mentally ill was needed, bringing forward the birth of asylums. On October 12, 1773, The United States' first asylum was founded in the city of Williamsburg, Virginia. Here, the Eastern State Hospital was built to be a solution to those suffering from mental illness. Very little treatment was provided, and the hospital eventually became more of a prison than a medical facility. Other asylums opening across the United States during this time followed this pattern.

Early in the 19th century, a new concept called "moral treatment" for the mentally ill began to make its way to the United States from Europe. The belief was that if someone was suffering from mental illness, they could potentially be cured if they were treated kindly and treatment was targeted to the rational part of the brain. Patients were removed from the sights and sounds of cities in the hope that peace and quiet would aid in recovery. As a result, new asylums were built out in the country, far from most of the population. Allentown State Hospital followed this pattern, located on a high piece of land with an entranceway of roughly 1,200 feet leading to the main building.

Dr. Thomas Story Kirkbride, superintendent of the Pennsylvania Hospital for the Insane, brought about another significant change for American asylums in the mid-19th century. As an advocate of mental health, he believed that those who suffered could be cured by consistent exposure to fresh air. Natural sunlight was also critical for a successful recovery. In order to achieve this, Kirkbride turned his focus on how asylums were designed and set out to establish an entirely new model for future asylums.

This new model came to be known as the "Kirkbride plan" and would go on to be used for the design of over 70 hospitals in the United States by 1910. A Kirkbride-style hospital was designed for a maximum of 250 patients, with a total of 71 employees—36 females and 35 males. Each staff member must either live in the hospital or in the immediate vicinity. Dr. Kirkbride also believed that the staff must be compensated fairly in order to retain the best talent in the field.

The layout would consist of the main core building with eight wings—four on the left and four on the right. Every wing would be staggered to allow all corridors to be exposed to sunlight and fresh air at both ends. A single wing would house a separate ward and be equipped with its own bathroom, clothes room, parlor, and infirmary. A patient's room was designed with high ceilings and was to house only one person at a time. When it came to the placement of the patients, the most extreme cases were housed in the farthest rooms out from the central building.

The Kirkbride plan did provide an improvement in the care of the mentally ill; however, around the 1890s, the state asylums became the target for local governments as a way to cut costs regarding almshouses and public hospitals. By redefining what was classified as a mental illness, they were able to shift a large population out of local facilities and into the state-run facilities. As a result, asylums designed for only 250 people were now holding thousands.

When Philip H. Johnson was assigned as the architect of Allentown State Hospital and began designing the institution around 1903, he roughly used Kirkbride's design for the hospital's layout. However, due to Johnson's lack of awareness of new concepts for institutions for the mentally ill, the hospital he laid out was already outdated. Medical professionals and advocates of the time began favoring other plans in accordance with new medical treatments of the 20th century.

Harrisburg State Hospital, an older sibling of Allentown State Hospital, was established in part by another well-known advocate of the 19th century, Dorothea Dix. Dix had a passion for teaching and began at the young age of 14. In 1819, she started a school for girls called the Dix Mansion along with a charity school that girls who came from poor families could attend for free. It was not until her early 40s that Dix started her crusade for mental health treatment reform.

In 1841, Dix had her most pivotal encounter with the standard of treatment for the mentally ill. A friend of hers was a Sunday school teacher at the East Cambridge Jail for Women and approached her about taking over the program, to which she obliged. What she saw when she entered the jail completely appalled her. Many of those who were deemed criminals were actually suffering from mental illness and had not even committed a crime. This type of inmate suffered the most and was even placed in cells without heat. Dix went directly to the local court, pushing for some to be released, and for updates to the facility. Though not completely successful, she was able to secure better living conditions for these inmates. This small victory launched a 40-year crusade to improve the treatment of the mentally ill.

Dix began investigating how other jails in the state treated their inmates and ended up drafting a document that was presented to the Massachusetts legislature. As a result, an increase in the budget for the state mental hospital at Worcester was approved, allowing the hospital to expand. For the next 40 years, Dorothea Dix traveled across the country campaigning for mental health reform. At the start of her crusade, there were only 13 mental hospitals in the country. By 1880, that number had risen to 123, with Dix having a direct effect on 32 of them. Her skills as a lobbyist earned her the label "voice for the mad" and she was regarded as the most politically active woman of the 19th century.

Dix's passion and drive paved the way for the development of the state institutions in Pennsylvania. She consistently lobbied for more institutions to care for the mentally ill, and as a result, the state hospital system built its first public insane asylum, Harrisburg State Hospital, in 1851. As time went on, Harrisburg, along with other cities in the state, became overcrowded, which led to the need for Allentown State Hospital.

Dorothea Dix was not the only one to step up for mental health reform. In 1887, American journalist Nellie Bly stepped into the spotlight when her book *10 Days in a Madhouse* was published. At the age of 23, Bly took an undercover assignment for the *New York World*, in which she had herself committed to Blackwell Island. She came up with a fake name and rented a room in a boardinghouse where she practiced acting ill in front of a mirror and then roamed the streets while yelling incoherently. Within a few days, the police were summoned and took Bly to be seen by a judge, where she claimed to be a Cuban immigrant suffering from amnesia.

Bly's first stop was at Bellevue Hospital, where she was diagnosed with dementia along with other illnesses of the mind. In the fall of 1887 she was sent to Blackwell Island, which housed an asylum built for 1,000 patients. When Bly arrived, there were over 1,600 patients and only 16 doctors on staff. For 10 days, she consumed rotten meat, contaminated water, and stale bread. If she resisted, she was threatened with physical punishment and the possibility of sexual violence. She underwent what was considered treatment, including freezing baths; soaking wet clothes; sitting on wooden benches for 12 hours or longer, unable to move or make a sound; and being tied together with other patients like cattle and forced to pull carts.

Bly was able to stay undercover for the full 10 days until her editor arranged for her release. Her article was published immediately and caused a media sensation, attracting the attention of a grand jury, which set out to visit the asylum. By the time they arrived at Blackwell Island, efforts had been made to cover up the abuse. These efforts failed, and the grand jury agreed with Bly. All abusive staff members were terminated and replaced. Since many of those who lived at the asylum were not actually mentally ill, but rather immigrants lost in the system, translators were brought in to assist. Finally, a new bill was introduced, providing $1 million in capital to improve the treatment of the mentally ill. An improved system for determining if a person was truly mentally ill or just in need of help was also established. Bly's efforts inspired other journalists to venture into asylums and expose corruption for decades to come.

Dr. Thomas Kirkbride, Dorothea Dix, and Nellie Bly are only a few examples of those courageous enough to challenge the mental health standards of the 19th century. Each had their own direct impact on shaping the world Allentown State Hospital was born into. This was only the beginning of state hospital reform. With the dawn of the 20th century, new challenges were on the horizon and a fresh generation of revolutionary thinkers kept change moving forward.

One
BUILDING PENNSYLVANIA'S FIRST HOMEOPATHIC STATE HOSPITAL

Christian Friedrich Samuel Hahnemann, the founder of homeopathy, was born on April 10, 1755, in Meissen, Saxony, which is now located in Germany. As a child, Hahnemann studied multiple languages including Latin, Greek, and Hebrew. His studies also expanded into history, physics, and botany. When he reached his early 20s, he began taking an interest in the study of medicine and attended the Universities of Leipzig, Vienna, and Erlangen. On August 10, 1779, at the age of 24, he received his medical degree from the University of Erlangen. (Courtesy of the Pennsylvania State Archives.)

Scottish physician William Cullen's work *A Treatise on the Materia Medica* is what exposed Hahnemann to the basic principles of what would eventually evolve into homeopathy. Hahnemann became familiar with Cullen's work around 1781, when he relocated to the village of Mansfeld, Saxony, to become the village's doctor. In 1784, Hahnemann gave up practicing medicine and made his living solely on translating and writing. While translating *A Treatise on the Materia Medica*, he came across the statement that cinchona (a type of Peruvian tree bark) was an acceptable treatment for malaria. (Courtesy of the Wellcome Collection.)

Hahnemann began experimenting on himself with cinchona to see how it would affect someone who was healthy. As a result of ingesting cinchona, Hahnemann claimed to experience many of the same symptoms malaria produced. It was at this moment he formed the idea that what causes a healthy person to have symptoms can be used to treat those same symptoms in an unhealthy person. Hahnemann coined the Latin term *similia similibus curentur*, which means "like cures like." When Edward Jenner discovered the smallpox vaccine in 1798, Hahnemann was convinced that this was even more proof that his theories were correct. (Courtesy of the Wellcome Collection.)

Dr. Henry Detweiler (pictured), William Wesselhoeft, Dr. John Eberhard Freitag, and Dr. John Romig are responsible for bringing homeopathy to the Lehigh Valley. Each of these men found their way to the practice of homeopathy with ease. The group created an informal school of homeopathy in Bath, Pennsylvania, at the home of Wesselhoeft in 1828 that ran from 1829 to 1835. The school was proving to be a success, and the physicians were looking to convert it into a degree-granting institution. In order to achieve this, the organization required a homeopath with an established reputation. Dr. Constantine Hering, a prominent European homeopath, had just arrived in Philadelphia and was a perfect fit for the institution. (Courtesy of the Pennsylvania State Archives.)

Known as "the father of American homeopathy," Constantine Hering first encountered homeopathy during his studies at the University of Leipzig. While performing an examination of a cadaver, he injured himself. The treatment at the time was amputation; however, Hering chose a homeopathic method and was healed. He became a strong advocate of Samuel Hahnemann and his work. Hering received his doctorate in medicine in 1826 from the University of Wurzburg. The homeopathic kit pictured here contained small amounts of animal, plant, synthetic, and mineral substances that would be diluted to a minute dose to treat an illness. (Author's collection.)

The cornerstone of the North American Academy of Homeopathic Healing Art at Allentown was laid on May 27, 1835, at 27–29 South Penn Street in Allentown. The academy ran from 1835 to 1839. On June 14, 1843, the Allentown Academy made a formal announcement declaring bankruptcy and closed its doors. The building was later purchased by the Allentown School District and demolished. Today, the school district's administration building sits at the site of the former academy. (Author's collection.)

Dr. Hering was determined to keep the study and lessons of homeopathy alive. In 1848, he, along with Dr. Jacob Jeanes and Dr. Walter Williamson, rented rooms in the back of a Philadelphia pharmacy and established the Homeopathic Medical College of Pennsylvania. The college started with only 15 students and 8 instructors. By 1869, the college changed its name to the Hahnemann Medical College of Philadelphia in honor of Dr. Samuel Hahnemann. (Courtesy of the Francis A. Countway Library.)

The Hahnemann Medical College of Philadelphia had many connections to Allentown State Hospital. When ASH opened its school for nurses in 1913, students were sent to the Hahnemann Hospital for three months to study medical and surgical nursing. Several of ASH's staff, including the first superintendent, Dr. Henry I. Klopp, and the second superintendent, Harry F. Hoffman (previously assistant superintendent), received their medical degrees from the Hahnemann Medical College and Hospital in Philadelphia. Dr. Klopp and Dr. Hoffman also lectured at Hahnemann Medical College during their tenure at ASH. (Author's collection.)

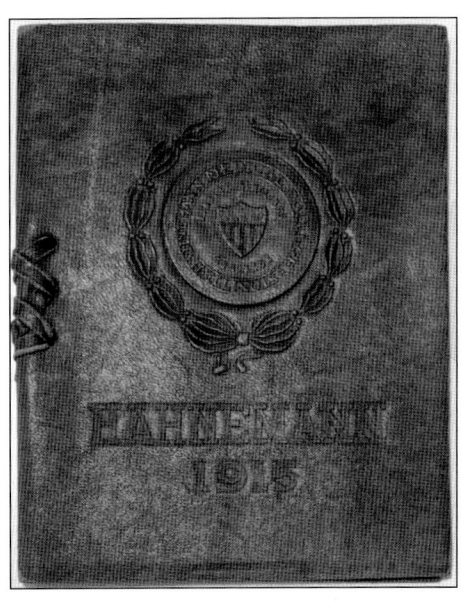

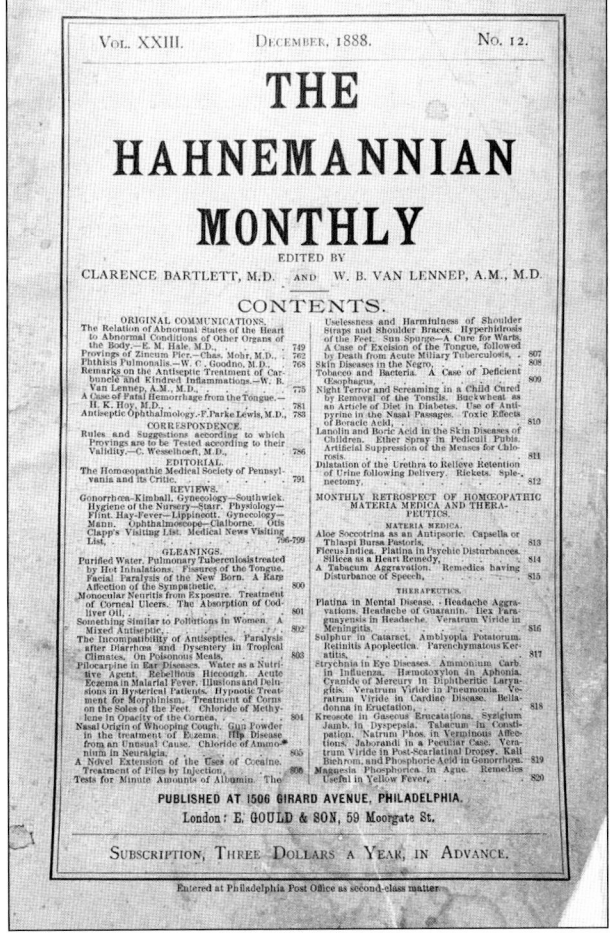

The Germantown Homœopathic Medical Society of Philadelphia was the driving force behind establishing the next state hospital as a homeopathic facility. In the mid-1890s, the society appointed a committee of 12 to introduce a bill to the state legislature to select land and construct a state hospital for the care of the mentally ill under homeopathic principles. Dr. Isaac W. Heysinger was appointed chairman with the purpose of pressuring the state to pass the bill. (Author's collection.)

At this time, there were five state institutions, including Danville State Hospital, that were suffering from overcrowding and not able to procure enough funds for expansion. In 1898, Dr. Heysinger called upon all the homeopathic societies in Pennsylvania to send delegates to work with the committee and secure passage by the legislature. (Author's collection.)

After many unsuccessful attempts, a bill was finally passed June 25–26, 1901, and a commission was assembled. The bill was titled "An Act to Provide for the Selection of a Site and the Erection of a State Hospital for the Treatment of the Insane Under Homoeopathic Management, to be Called the Homoeopathic State Hospital for the Insane, and Making an Appropriation Therefor." (Author's collection.)

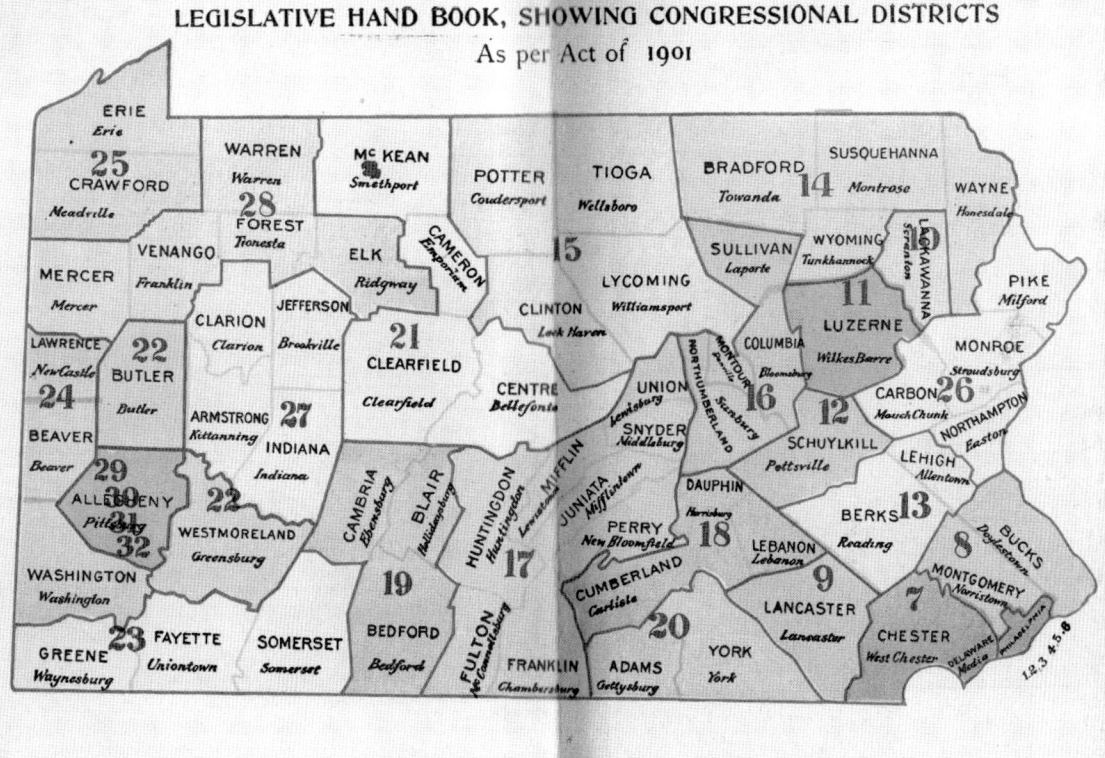

The bill instructed that a plot of land should be selected somewhere near the center of the populations of Bradford, Bucks, Carbon, Lackawanna, Lehigh, Monroe, Northampton, Pike, Sullivan, Susquehanna, Wayne, and Wyoming Counties. The land needed to be arable with an adequate supply of water nearby. An allowance of $300,000 of state revenue was set as the maximum purchase price. On July 18, 1901, Gov. William A. Stone approved the bill except for Section 5, which covered the $300,000 allowance to purchase land and begin construction. This was due to insufficient state funds. (Author's collection.)

Dr. Heysinger, before receiving any proposals on land, took a map of Pennsylvania and determined the center point of the counties to be between Allentown and Bethlehem. Taking his map, he traveled to Allentown to visit J.D. Newhard, his only connection to the city. Together, the two men set out and identified the point that Dr. Heysinger had marked on his map as the farm of Robert E. Wright. Impressed with the land, closeness of the railroad, and access to water, Dr. Heysinger felt this was the ideal location. There were several other proposed sites, and in December 1902, the commissioners set out to visit sites in Lehigh, Northampton, Monroe, Bradford, and Wayne Counties. After viewing all available sites, three in Lehigh County were under consideration until a final decision was made to purchase 209 acres of land in Rittersville, Pennsylvania. This land included the estates of Robert E. Wright, J. Marshall Wright, and others for approximately $40,000. (Courtesy of the Library of Congress.)

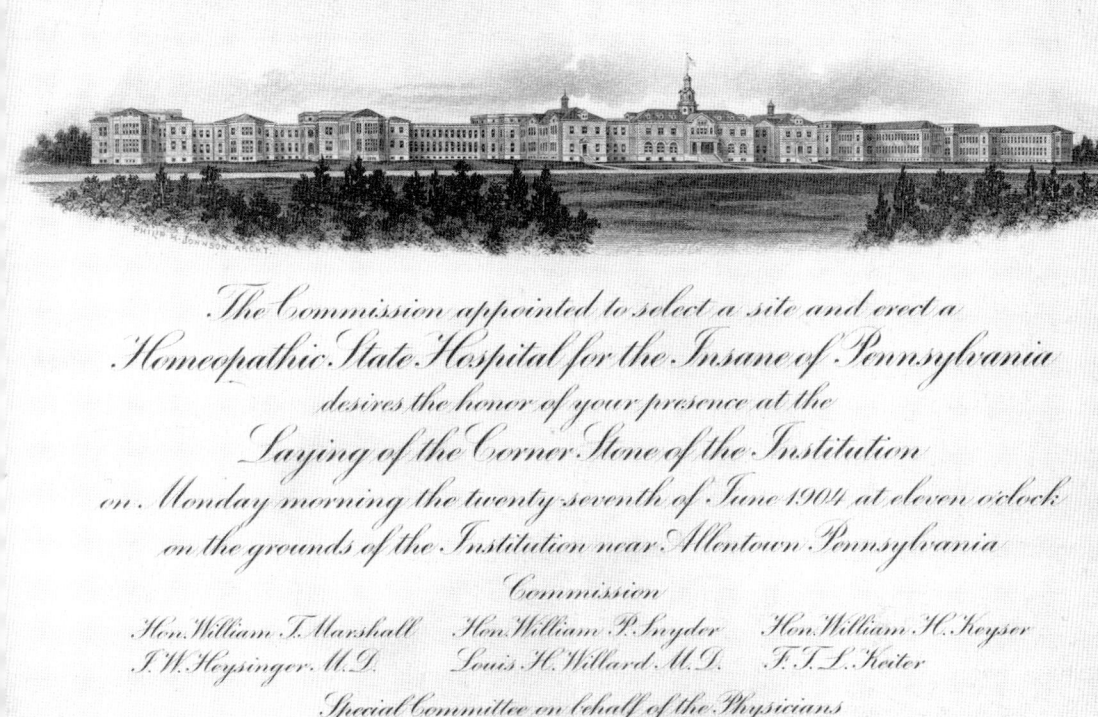

On June 27, 1904, around 11:00 a.m., a ceremony was conducted for the laying of the cornerstone. Special trains ran from Philadelphia and Harrisburg directly to the Allentown terminal. The Lehigh Valley Traction Company provided the car *Electra* to the governor, as well as eight trolley cars to take all arriving parties directly to the hospital grounds. Many prominent politicians and physicians were present for the ceremony, including Dr. C.M. Thomas, the dean of Hahnemann Hospital. Gov. Samuel W. Pennypacker gave the chief address, which included talks about the change and evolution of the care for the mentally ill. Dr. McClellan followed with a speech on the history of homeopathy in the Lehigh Valley noting the North American Academy of Homoeopathic Healing Art as being the first college of homeopathy in America. (Courtesy of Shawn McClure.)

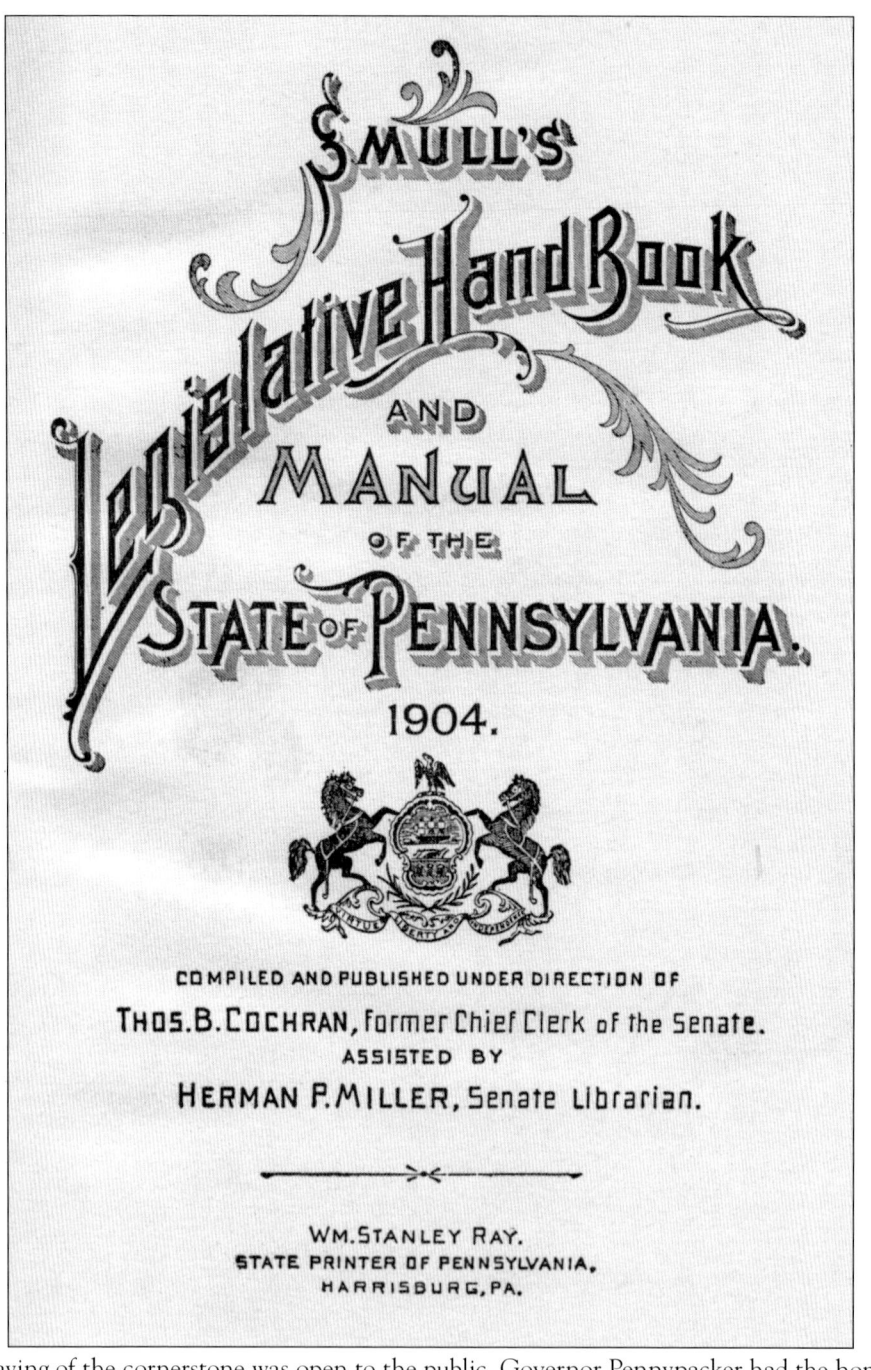

The laying of the cornerstone was open to the public. Governor Pennypacker had the honor of performing the ceremony and placed the cornerstone at the northeast corner of building B, the east end wing. Made out of Maine granite, the stone included a small depression reserved for a time capsule. The face of the stone had the year "1904" countersunk into it. The time capsule was a waterproof copper box containing Smull's handbook, a copy of the act creating the commission, a list of the invited guests, the day's newspaper, and the names of the national and state officials. (Author's collection.)

It took roughly 11 years for the hospital to be built, mainly due to Governor Stone failing to approve the allowance covered in section 5 of the initial bill. On May 10, 1911, Gov. John K. Tener approved an amendment to the original law of 1901. As a result, an entirely new commission had to be appointed along with funds. Finally, the institution was completed in 1912. (Courtesy of Gregory Smith.)

The above photograph was taken on July 1, 1908, from the southwest corner of the property, looking northeast at the foundation of the auditorium in its beginning stages of construction. Below is a view of the auditorium close to being complete, taken from the southeast corner in March 1911. The total cost for the purchase of land and construction of buildings came out to $1,931,270. The farmland on the hospital grounds cost approximately $58,000. The buildings, including the electric plant and power system, came to $1,821,000. The rest of the costs went to the pumping station and water reservoir. (Both, courtesy of Gregory Smith.)

This is the hospital's boiler house on March 24, 1911, near the end of construction. As the hospital expanded, a need for a more efficient system was required. In 1932, the system was replaced with three 600-horsepower boilers along with a new stack and flue. (Courtesy of Gregory Smith.)

Many state hospitals participated in what was known at the time as "occupational therapy." Patients who were capable of working produced goods either for the hospital or to sell. Fairview State Hospital in Waymart, Pennsylvania, had its own brick-making factory and produced many of the bricks used to build Allentown State Hospital. (Courtesy of Gregory Smith.)

These two images show the industrial building from the early stages of construction to completion. For the next couple of years, buildings would be revised to make up for the increase in patients and the equipment required to maintain the property. (Both, courtesy of Gregory Smith)

The above image shows buildings A, B, and C completed. Construction of the corridors continues, connecting the center hub to the first two wards. By the time the hospital reached its peak population, these corridors would be lined with patient beds. The image below shows ward building M. (Both, courtesy of Gregory Smith.)

Philip H. Johnson was the architect responsible for the design of Allentown State Hospital. Johnson was brother-in-law to Israel W. Durham, a Republican state senator who held a vast amount of political power in Philadelphia. In 1903, Durham helped secure Johnson a contract giving him a monopoly over any architectural work of the Department of Health and Charities for the rest of Johnson's career. Johnson's contract also secured for himself five percent of all the cost of buildings and fixtures. (Author's collection.)

Due to the substantial delay of construction, by the time the hospital was finally built, it was significantly outdated compared to the new standards of treatment for the mentally ill. Expectations for the hospital were for the facility to hold 5,000 patients; however, the completed hospital could only hold 1,000 beds. (Courtesy of the Pennsylvania State Archives.)

Once complete, the hospital was turned over to the board of trustees. After reviewing many candidates, Dr. Henry I. Klopp, assistant superintendent of the Westborough State Hospital in Massachusetts, was the final choice by the board of trustees. He was officially appointed superintendent of Allentown State Hospital on February 17, 1912, with an annual salary of $5,000. (Courtesy of the Allentown Public Library.)

Dr. Klopp attended the Hahnemann Medical College and Hospital in Philadelphia and graduated in 1894, second in his class. His first year working in medicine was at the Reading Homeopathic Hospital, where he served as a resident physician. In 1895, Klopp resigned from Reading to take a position at Westborough State Hospital. (Author's collection.)

The decision to choose Dr. Klopp as superintendent was backed by a number of recommendations praising his abilities. Klopp was already making changes at Westborough that were gaining traction, and when the news of his resignation reached Massachusetts state officials, a counteroffer was made for a considerable increase in salary, which he declined. At the age of 42, Klopp made the move to Allentown. (Courtesy of Westborough Public Library.)

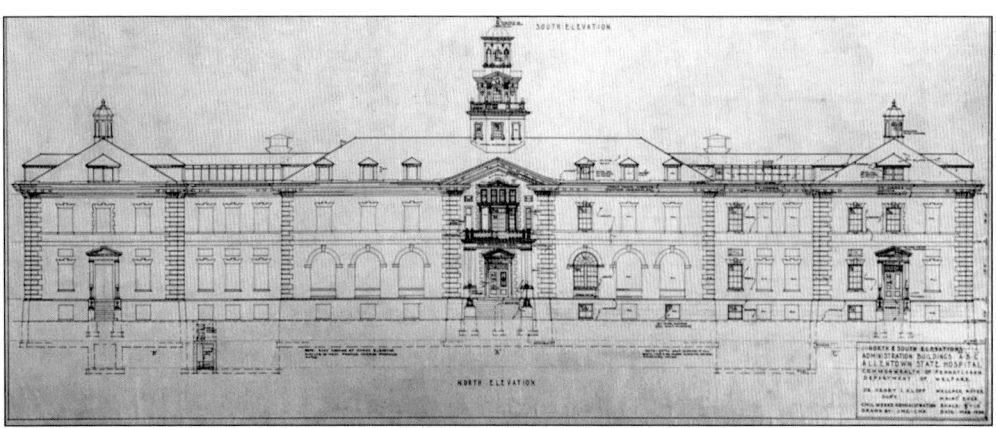

These are the blueprints for the administration building. This building, composed of 30-inch-thick walls, was broken into three parts, all connected by an underground seven-foot-wide tunnel. The center structure, known as building A, contained the offices of the superintendent, resident physician, and his assistants. The supply clerk, drug room, and the steward and recording rooms were also here. (Courtesy of the Pennsylvania State Archives.)

The most impressive part of building A is the rotunda and entranceway seen here, composed of marble and tile. Buildings B and C included rooms for supervisors, assistant physicians, nurses, and clerks, plus detention rooms and receiving rooms for patients. (Courtesy of Gregory Smith.)

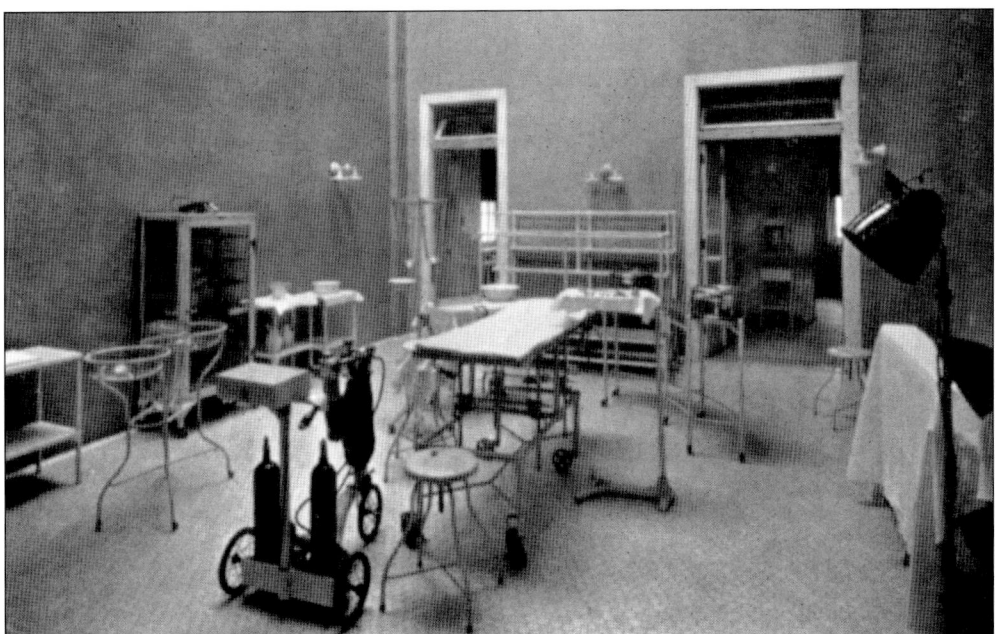

Expanding out from the administration building were four ward buildings, an operating room (pictured here), a building for staff dining, two chapels, an auditorium, a laundry building, a boiler, a kitchen, an ice- and cold-storage plant, and a power and electric plant. (Courtesy of the Allentown Public Library.)

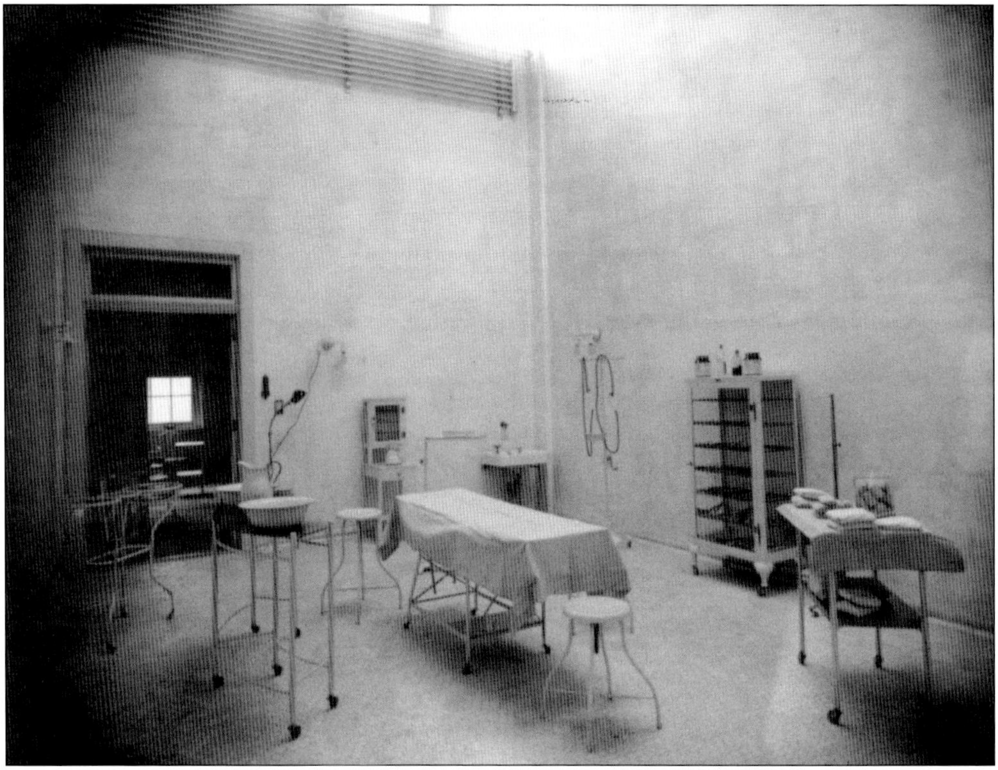

The image above shows the exam room for the hospital, while below is the post-operation room. From February 19 to March 25, 1912, Dr. Klopp toured these buildings taking notes and compiling an inventory to furnish the hospital. By May 1912, it was determined that 50,000 furnishings were needed, including 1,200 beds, 1,200 mattresses, 2,500 pillows, 6,000 plates, and 8,000 spoons. The board of trustees allowed companies to bid on these items. Because of the primitive layout of the hospital, changes had to be made, including to the buildings' arrangements. This contract was awarded to Doyle & Co. for $8,750. (Both, courtesy of Gregory Smith.)

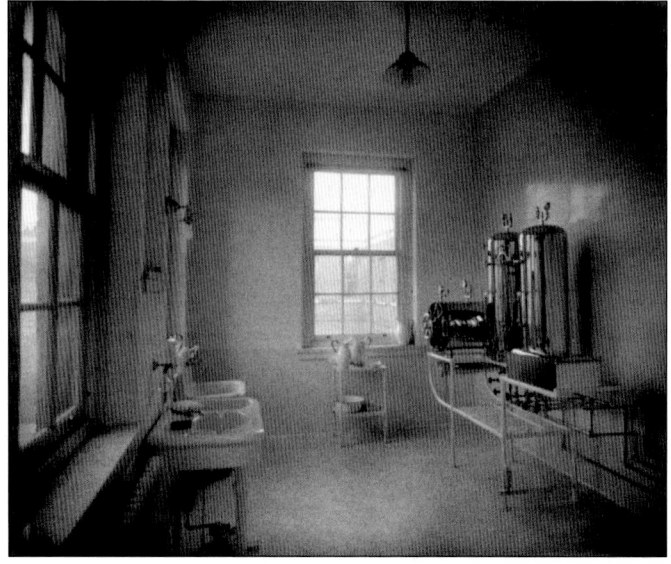

In May 1912, the hospital was opened for tours. On one Sunday, roughly 4,000 people came. Many asked to see the padded cells, to which Dr. Henry Klopp responded, "Padded cells won't cure people afflicted with mental derangement. The purpose of asylum treatment is to relieve and cure the unfortunates. The treatment will not be violent, but humane and remedial. " Klopp viewed the facility as a hospital for the mind and even refused to use the hospital's embossing stamp because it had the words "insane asylum." (Both, courtesy of Gregory Smith.)

Pictured here is the hospital's bakery. From May 31, 1913, to May 31, 1914, the hospital spent $69,235.17 on groceries. This included meat, flour, butter, eggs, milk, yeast, fruits, and vegetables. In an attempt to cut costs, the hospital would eventually produce all these on its own farm. (Courtesy of Gregory Smith.)

This is the auditorium, which remained up to the closure of the hospital. It was not uncommon for the hospital to host plays, talent shows, music, and even pageants. Other hospitals would hold events here as well. (Courtesy of Gregory Smith.)

Two
THE EPOCH-MAKING YEARS

Dr. Henry I. Klopp is pictured here in 1914. Dr. Klopp had a New England accent, and was known as a progressive thinker dedicated to his patients and always open to new concepts and ideas. He also lived by his slogan, "Unless you get happiness out of your work, you will never know what real happiness is." Behind him on top of his desk is a small bust of Dr. Samuel Hahnemann. (Courtesy of the Pennsylvania State Archives.)

Allentown State Hospital officially opened its doors to receive patients on October 3, 1912, as the first homeopathic state hospital in Pennsylvania. Patients were transferred from five facilities to Allentown, with a majority coming from Norristown State Hospital or Danville State Hospital. The first 50 patients came from Norristown. Harrisburg State Hospital sent one man and one woman, Wernersville State Asylum sent one woman, and Philadelphia County Hospital sent one woman. From October 3, 1912, to February 1, 1913, the total number of patients was 750. (Above, courtesy of the Painter/Reese family; below, author's collection.)

Dr. Klopp was granted the ability to hire his own staff. This 1914 photograph shows assistant superintendent Dr. Harry Hoffman in his office in building A. Dr. Hoffman graduated from the University of Buffalo in 1906 and received his medical degree from Hahnemann college in 1910. He would later go on to be the assistant physician at Norwich State Hospital in Connecticut from 1910 until his departure to Allentown State Hospital in 1912. Hoffman lived in the staff quarters with his family and had a reputation for being a quiet man and a deep thinker. (Courtesy of the Pennsylvania State Archives.)

Dr. Walter Lang was recruited by Dr. Hoffman from the Easton Sanatorium to serve as Allentown State Hospital's senior assistant physician. He was regarded by the board of trustees as overqualified and eventually left Allentown to join the US Army, where he rose to the rank of major in the Medical Corps. After his discharge, Dr. Lang became the superintendent of Westborough State Hospital from 1919 to 1946. (Courtesy of the Pennsylvania State Archives.)

William J. Leahy (above) came to Allentown State Hospital from Norwich, Connecticut, in 1912. He was the supervisor of the men's department and retired as a hospital steward in 1947. Tirza R. McGinnes, supervisor of nurses, and her assistant, Ms. Sullivan, are seen below. Supervisors had their offices in building B or C. Both photographs were taken in 1914 by pathologist Dr. Charles B. Reitz and donated to the hospital in 1994 by his daughter Ruth (Reitz) Balish. (Both, courtesy of the Pennsylvania State Archives.)

Charles W. Fritchmann served as the hospital's steward from 1912 to 1921. Fritchmann previously served at Trenton State Hospital. In 1921, while leaving a trolley car in front of the hospital, Fritchman was struck by an automobile and suffered severe injuries. He was immediately taken inside to the surgery room; however, after hours in critical condition, he passed away. (Courtesy of the Pennsylvania State Archives.)

Mary Leymaster Served as Dr. Henry Klopp's private secretary and confidential stenographer. Dr. Klopp often called Leymaster a "gem" of a secretary because of how efficient she was. She served as the hospital stenographer from 1912 to 1931. (Courtesy of the Allentown Public Library.)

Mary H. Murray was a graduate of the Allentown State Hospital Nurses Training School in 1921. The year after her graduation, she was promoted to the position of director of nurses. Murray was also assisted by nurse Elinor T. Cotellis. The image below shows Murray and Cotellis's office. The nurse training school at Allentown State Hospital was established in 1913 and ran until 1936. Murray served as director of nurses from 1922 to 1925. (Both, courtesy of the Allentown Public Library.)

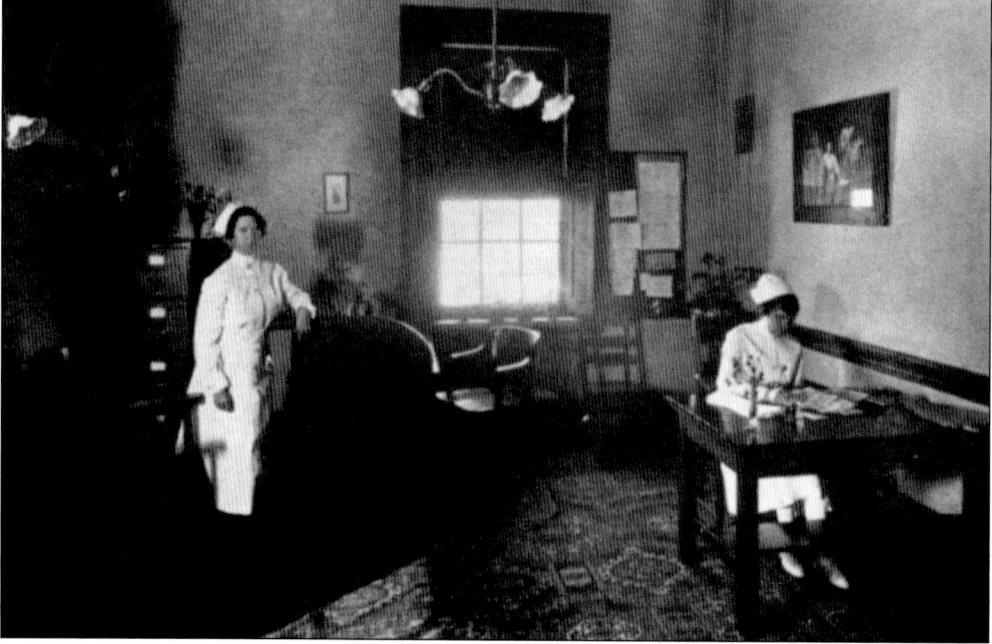

The above photograph shows the graduating class of 1925. While attending the training school, students were exposed to a variety of classes, including special therapeutics, communicable diseases, chemistry, anatomy, homeopathy, anatomy, bacteriology, and emergency nursing. The one-year program was broken into 63 days of medical, 84 days of surgical, 60 days of pediatrics, 84 days of obstetrics, 56 days of operating room training, and 18 vacation days. From 1916 to 1937, a total of 189 nurses graduated from the Allentown State Hospital Nurses Training School. (Above, courtesy of the Pennsylvania State Archives; below, courtesy of Gregory Smith.)

Still suffering from a lack of funds, the board of trustees submitted a multitude of complaints to the state Board of Public Charities. Two major complaints noted in the annual report of 1912 to 1914 were about the hospital grounds not being maintained. Gov. John Tener did not approve

a budget for the expansion of the hospital grounds or the roads of the facility, which the board of trustees went on to state would be "beneficial both to the patients and their visiting friends." (Courtesy of the Pennsylvania State Archives.)

Dr. Henry Klopp's ideal hospital was to serve two main functions. If an individual was deemed "incurable," the hospital should provide a safe haven. Those who have the potential for being cured should be provided treatment in a hospital setting with a goal of discharge. Dr. Klopp believed that in order for the hospital to be most effective, the mentally ill would have to be separated into three divisions: the acute and curable, chronic cases that require strict supervision, and the chronic but harmless. Klopp's first annual report covering 1912 to 1914 stated that dormitory-style living was not the best solution for treatment. (Courtesy of the Painter/Reese family.)

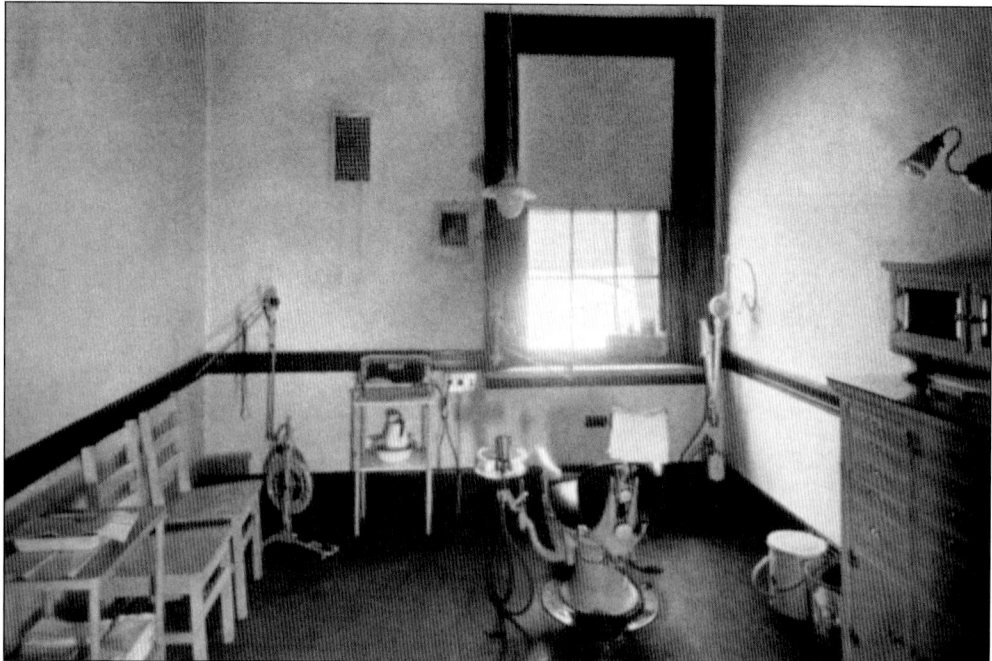

In August 1913, the hospital was able to hire a local dentist to come one day each week. He would see as many patients as possible, performing extractions, fillings, cleanings, and more. If a patient had the funds, he would also make dentures for them. (Courtesy of the Allentown Public Library.)

Dr. Klopp noted in his second report to the board of trustees (pictured) that "since the beginning of 1915 the hospital has been crowded and exceeding bed capacity." As a result of the overcrowding, Klopp reached out to the other state hospitals, asking them to confirm that there was a vacancy before sending a patient. The Committee on Lunacy of the Board of Public Charities pushed back on Klopp and Allentown State Hospital by declaring that "if the hospital has sufficient accommodations to care for a greater number of patients than what comes from its own districts, then more patients can be sent from other facilities." Klopp would continue to stress that Allentown State Hospital was not a place to pack as many people in as possible. It was a hospital for the mentally ill, which provided therapy for people to return to society and their families as quickly as possible. (Courtesy of the Allentown Public Library.)

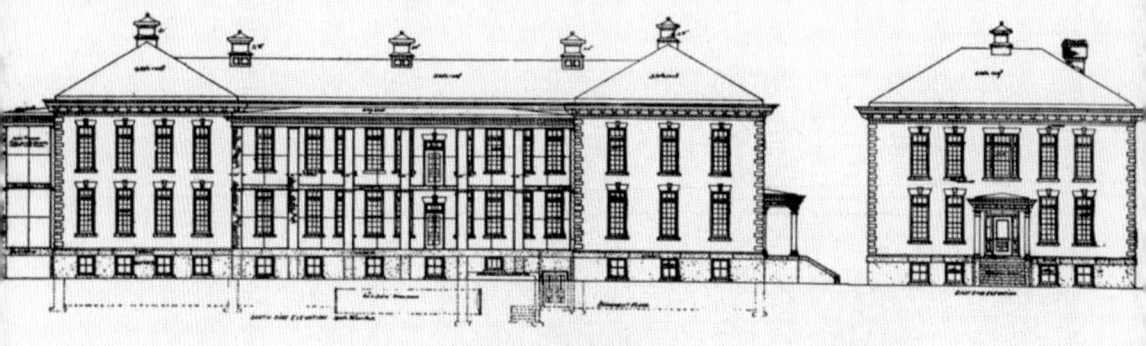

RECEPTION BUILDING

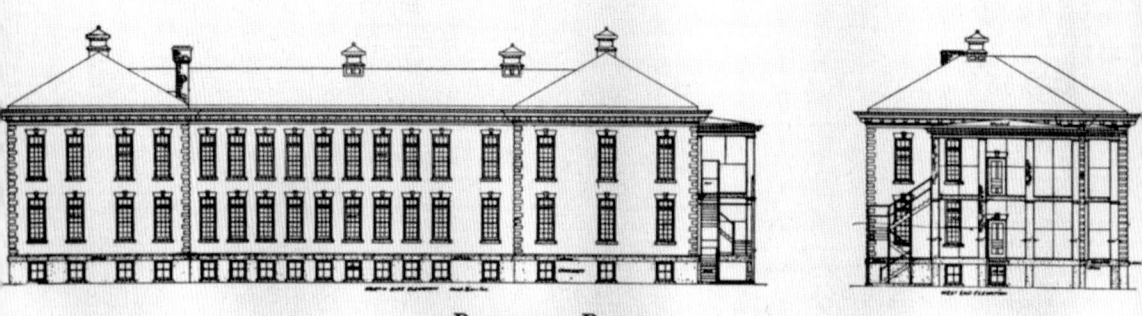

RECEPTION BUILDING

The need for rapid expansion was evident in the very first official report. Dr. Henry Klopp recommended to the board of trustees that they apply for the following in the special appropriations of the upcoming 1915 legislature: a reception building, a nurses' home for women, two buildings to provide for nurses' and attendants' dining rooms with second-floor quarters for employees, a double house for farm employees, an industrial building for male patients, a garage and repair shop, and seven improvements including safety devices. This is the architect's sketch of the reception building Dr. Klopp had requested to be built on the campus so they could properly classify patients before admitting them to the hospital. (Courtesy of the Allentown Public Library.)

The year 1916 was very productive for the hospital. Skilled staff had increased to six physicians. Construction projects were well underway, including tuberculous pavilions, reducing the risk of the disease spreading throughout the hospital. The white building at left was one of the tuberculous buildings on campus. Another construction project, the first of the hospital's psychiatric institute division buildings (building RV) opened for female patients that year as well. (Courtesy of the Pennsylvania State Archives.)

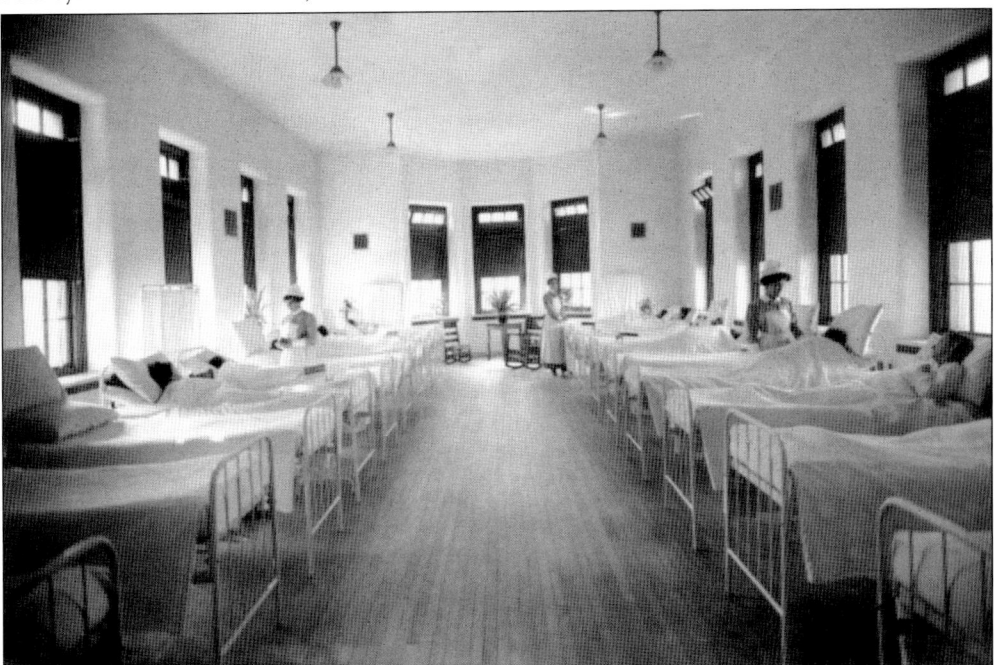

With the outbreak of World War I, Allentown State Hospital experienced a shortage of skilled staff. Administration became disorganized, and annual reports were discontinued until 1922. Influenza plagued the hospital in 1918 and 1919, causing many of the staff to become ill and bedridden. At one point, only two physicians were well enough to take care of patients. (Courtesy of Gregory Smith.)

Music programs at Allentown State Hospital proved to be therapeutic to patients. In 1922, Dr. William Van De Wall (seated at the piano) established a theoretical and practical music program for state mental institutions. From 1923 to 1926, he ran the music program at the hospital until it was fully established and was turned over to Lois Hannaford on December 30, 1926. Hanford went on to grow the program even further by developing a chorus and orchestra and holding seasonal pageants and concerts for the patients. (Author's collection.)

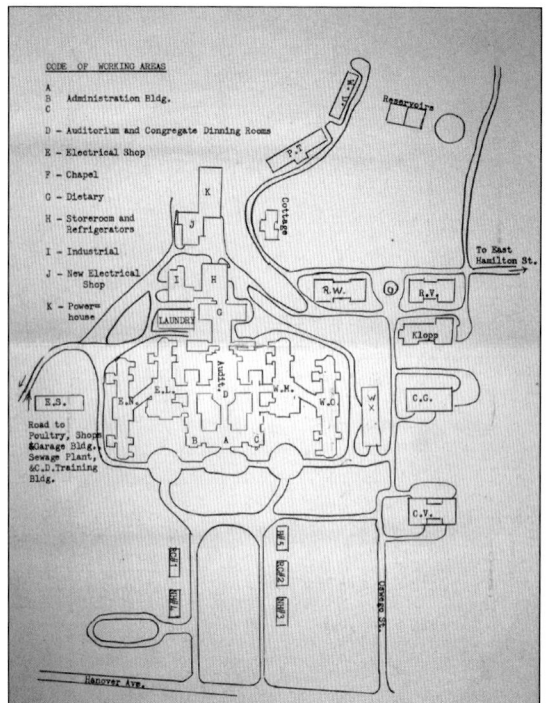

In November 1924, the hospital opened the second of its psychiatric institute division buildings known as the RW building. By 1924, the hospital had a total of nine physicians, and roughly 500 patients were being admitted annually. By the end of the first quarter-century of the hospital's existence, a total of 9,739 people had been admitted. (Courtesy of the Pennsylvania State Archives.)

Three
FARM LIFE AND THE WEAVERSVILLE COLONIES

Farm manager John McDevitt is operating a tractor with a fertilization wagon attached. McDevitt worked on the farm from 1968 to its closure in 1981. Up until the Peonage Abolishment Act of 1974, patients worked alongside him as a form of therapy. McDevitt was one of the last workers to leave the farm and transfer to the main campus, where he served as fire marshal from 1981 to 1984 and then director of safety and security from 1984 to 2004. (Courtesy of John McDevitt.)

From 1912 to April 1917, all farming operations were conducted on 105 of the 214 acres at the main hospital grounds in Rittersville, Pennsylvania. In the first annual report to the board of trustees, the grounds are described as "only suitable, under intensive cultivation, for trucking and dairying." Male patients worked for the first two years clearing underbrush, cutting down trees, removing rocks and stones, removing old fences, and building a dairy barn. Existing structures were used to house livestock but were inefficient due to their scattered locations on the property. (Courtesy of the Painter/Reese family.)

By the end of 1916, all farm buildings had been centralized, with the exception of a home for the farm manager. Dr. Henry Klopp applied for special appropriations from the 1917 legislature to be able to construct a new farmhouse, an industrial building to house 50 male patients who worked on the farm, and an addition to the piggery. In order to adequately provide for the growing facility, Dr. Klopp also requested the funds to purchase an additional 500 acres. (Courtesy of the Painter/Reese family.)

In 1916, the City of Allentown purchased the Geisinger farm in Rittersville, Pennsylvania, with the intent of building a sewage treatment plant. Only needing about 60 acres, the city determined it could sell or lease the remaining land. Allentown State Hospital's president of the board of trustees, Col. Harry C. Trexler, secured a year-long lease of the farm from April 1917 to March 31, 1918, for $700. Unfortunately, the land consisted of depleted soil and overgrown weeds, forcing the hospital to look elsewhere for farmland. (Author's collection.)

In 1919, the legislature granted a special appropriation for the purchase of farmland. The hospital purchased 140 acres plus 10 acres of a wood lot for $22,000 in the historic Scotch/Irish-Presbyterian settlement in East Allen Township, Northampton County, known as Weaversville. This section was known as State Farm Colony No. 1. An old stagecoach stop on the land was converted to house 18 male patients and caretakers. (Courtesy of Collis Truck Parts.)

A second plot of farmland consisting of 121 acres of the Deshler farm (Farm Colony No. 2) and Brown farm (Farm Colony No. 3) was purchased as a result of an appropriation granted in 1919. Here, an additional eight patients could be housed in the Deshler home, including their caretakers. This area would be known as State Farm Colony No. 2. Between 1930 and 1932, the hospital, through special appropriation, purchased two additional farms and a parcel of land in Weaversville, adding 319 acres to the already existing farmland. (Courtesy of John McDevitt.)

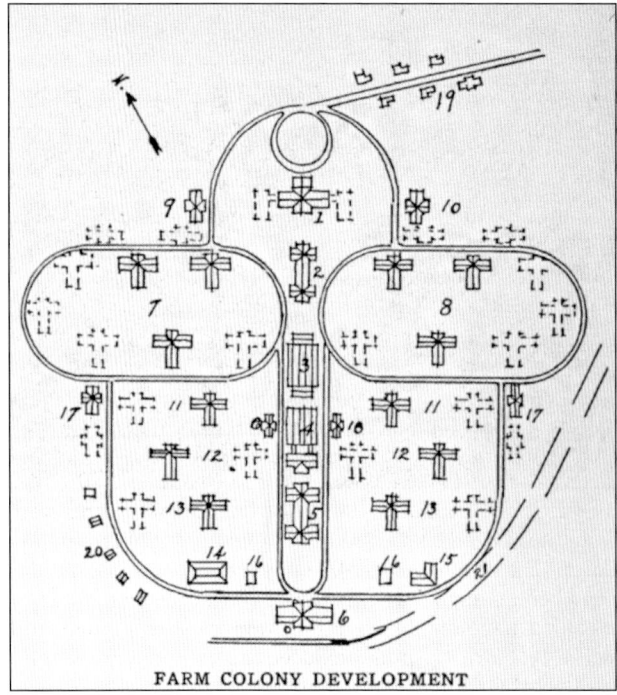

In 1936, a study focused on anticipated population growth over the next 30 years was conducted at the farm colonies in Weaversville. The end goal was the construction and development of an Allentown State Hospital annex campus. Dr. Henry Klopp strongly favored the cottage plan versus the Kirkbride plan due to his belief that patients would benefit far more from small groups than large wards. In the 1936 annual report, Dr. Klopp submitted a layout of his vision for the campus that could accommodate 2,000 future patients. Though the hospital's population continued to grow, this vision would never come to fruition. (Courtesy of the Pennsylvania State Archives.)

Since the hospital opened in 1912, Dr. Henry Klopp had continually requested funds for expansion. In 1937, the General State Authority Board allocated $1,387,925 to Allentown State Hospital for the construction of additional buildings. The Weaversville Farm Colony would see the construction of a dormitory for 85 men, dairy barns, four silos, two haykeepers, two storage sheds, a bullpen, a hog house, a manure pit, and a garage. The total cost for these additions was $259,459. (Courtesy of the Pennsylvania State Archives.)

Dairy products were an export of Allentown State Hospital and were distributed among other state institutions, including Farview, Retreat, White Haven, Clark Summit, Hamburg, and Wernersville. In 1937, the hospital produced 668,358 pounds of milk. By 1942, construction and installation of equipment at the new dairy barns had been completed. On August 20 of that year, all dairy cattle were relocated to the dairy barns at Farm Colony No. 3. Production was streamlined, and dairy production rates continued to rise. In 1958, the hospital produced the most amount of milk per cow of all state institutions. (Courtesy of the Pennsylvania State Archives.)

Additional challenges were presented by the management of the dairy herd. Cattle were consistently at risk and checked for diseases such as Bang's disease, mastitis, tuberculosis, and keratitis. In order to produce the largest amount of milk, Allentown State Hospital would keep bulls on the farm in the bullpen seen here or rent purebred bulls from local farmers for breeding. By 1943, artificial insemination was introduced through a contract with Lehigh Valley Cooperative Farms, reducing the need to keep a population of bulls for breeding. (Courtesy of the Pennsylvania State Archives.)

This is the hog house on Farm Colony No. 3 on September 20, 1939. Allentown State Hospital held a contract with A&B Meats, which would slaughter the livestock and send the remains to the main campus. Since 1913, pork has served as one of the hospital's most profitable products. For the year ending May 31, 1915, the hospital had produced 7,761 pounds of pork products. By 1951, that number had risen to around 72,000 pounds per year. (Courtesy of the Pennsylvania State Archives.)

Allentown State Hospital's goal was to be as self-sufficient as possible, producing a majority of its food at the farm colonies of Weaversville. Besides meat and dairy production, a variety of fruits and vegetables were grown at the hospital's farm. Occasionally, the hospital would participate in state competitions, showcasing its best crops and livestock. In 1930, superintendent Dr. Henry Klopp received the title "Potato King of Pennsylvania" after the hospital farm produced 2,690 bushels of potatoes on a five-acre plot. (Author's collection.)

Silos are being constructed on Farm Colony No. 3. By 1942, Farm Colony No. 3 was completed and ready to be used. Unfortunately, the farm faced a new challenge of obtaining enough skilled labor. Due to World War II, the hospital lost many of its physical laborers to the military. Others left the hospital to pursue better-paying farm work in the area. As a result, farm production decreased. (Courtesy of the Pennsylvania State Archives.)

In 1941, the board of trustees determined that the farm colonies should no longer be referred to as Farm Colony Nos. 1, 2, and 3. New names were based on the region and history of the area. Farm Colony No. 1 was changed to the Horner Colony after Jane Horner, who was killed and scalped by Indians a few miles away from the site in 1763, according to her gravestone seen above. Farm Colony No. 2 became the Deschler and Brown Farm after revolutionary war hero Gen. Robert Brown. Farm Colony No. 3 became Dechheim Colony after the family that previously owned the land. (Above, author's collection; below, courtesy of the Pennsylvania State Archives.)

On April 30, 1973, Senate Bill 731, also known as the Peonage Abolishment Act, was introduced and approved to go into effect on January 1, 1974. Those patients who enjoyed being part of the farm colony or participated in occupational therapy were no longer allowed to work or perform chores at the hospital without being paid. Many patients had a negative reaction to the change. Eventually, all patients were transferred to the main campus, and the once profitable farm was now barely able to break even. (Both, courtesy of the Pennsylvania State Archives.)

After the transfer of patients back to the main campus, the state converted the farm dormitory into a juvenile detention facility for minors. The Center for Community Alternatives (also known as Camp Hill Project), a nonprofit corporation, was funded by the state to manage the facility and opened its doors on October 10, 1975. Within a month, four juveniles had escaped, causing a public outcry in the area. East Allen Township officials attempted to close the center, but failed. Over its 25-year lifespan, the state-contracted detention facility was run by various organizations. In May 2010, the facility was closed and abandoned. (Above, courtesy of the Pennsylvania State Archives; below, author's collection.)

By 1980, all state school and state hospital farms were closed by the state Department of Public Welfare. Allentown State Hospital's farm remained open until 1981 to facilitate the sale of all assets. In March 1981, the farm's entire dairy herd was auctioned. Previous staff members were either laid off or returned to the main campus to fill gaps in staffing. (Both, courtesy of John McDevitt.)

In 1997, state officials divided the remaining farmland to be auctioned off. This sale included the last remaining homes of the Craig Settlement, the Lehigh Valley's oldest settlement, which sat upon the grounds of a prehistoric Indian village. Jaindl Turkey Farms purchased 370 acres with the intent to use the land for farming. East Allen Township purchased 29 acres to expand Bicentennial Park and an additional 11.6 acres, which contained the dairy barns. In the summer of 2011, the township demolished the remaining structures on the 11.6 acres. In 2017, the township purchased additional acres, which contained the juvenile detention facility (previously the dormitory of Farm Colony No. 3) with the intent to demolish the structure and replace it with a public works building. (Courtesy of John McDevitt.)

Four

BUILDING FOR THE FUTURE

Allentown State Hospital was dedicated to fire safety throughout its years of operation. Taken in 1925, this image showcases the state hospital's fire apparatus sitting in front of the carpenter shop. In the 1960s and 1970s, the hospital had its own rescue squad that would aid in community disasters. In 1973, the squad was disbanded due to one of the members suffering a heart attack while responding to an apartment fire. (Courtesy of the Pennsylvania State Archives.)

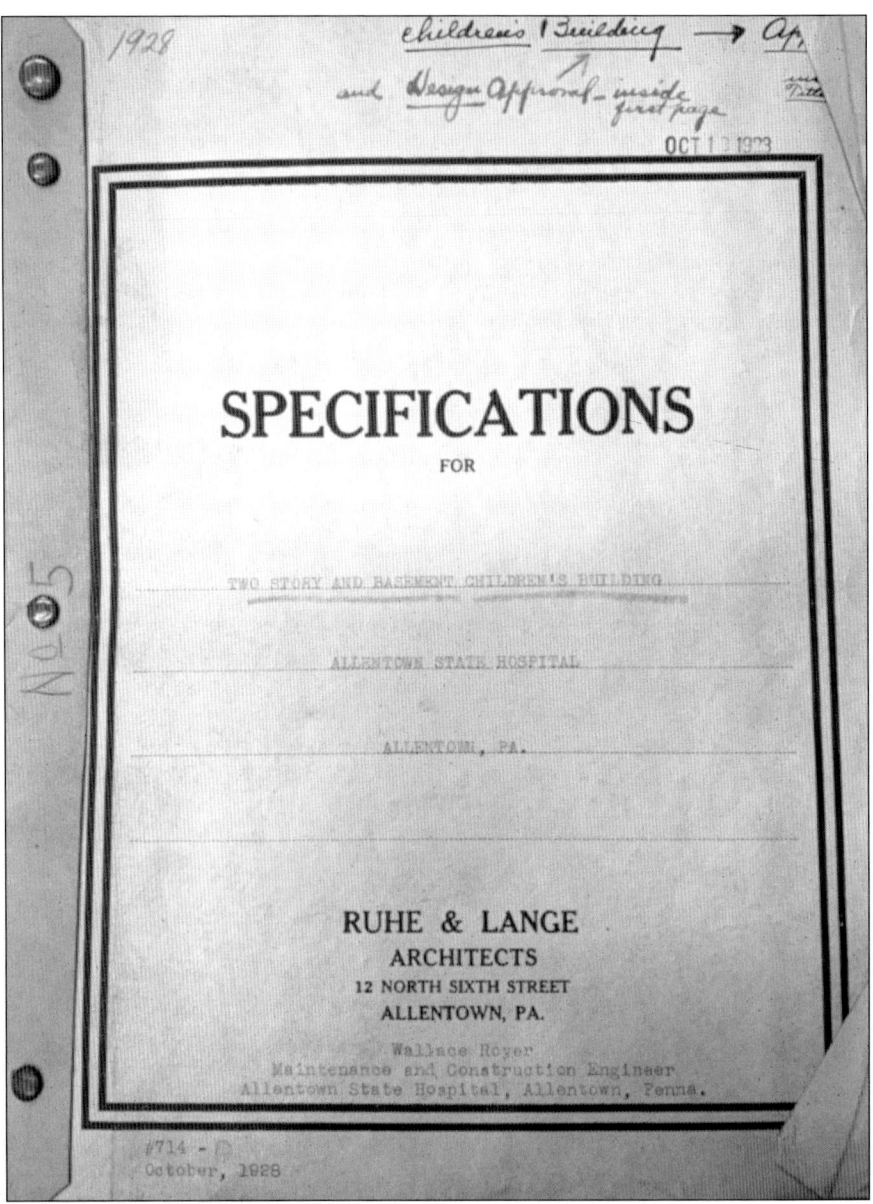

In the mid-1920s, Dr. . Klopp began taking an interest in the concept of separating children from the adult patients of the hospital. During this period, children were mixed in with adults, and providing adequate care was difficult and sometimes impossible. In his 1926 report to the board of trustees, Dr. Klopp stressed the need for children to be separated, and in 1928, the hospital opened up bids on a new two-story building to house children. Working closely with construction engineer Wallace Royer, Klopp designed the building to the standards he wanted to provide. In 1930, the unit opened and soon attracted leading psychiatrists from around the world, including Dr. Mildred Creak. Funded by the Rockefeller Fellowship Award, Dr. Creak came to America from London to study Klopp's new children's building. What she learned from two years at Allentown she took back and began establishing similar services throughout the United Kingdom. In 1932, Klopp published his research and findings on the effectiveness of the children's building in the *American Journal of Psychiatry*. (Courtesy of the Pennsylvania State Archives.)

During its final stages of construction, Dr. Klopp spared no expense when it came to furnishing and providing leading medical care of the time in the children's building. Some of the distinctive features of the building included a swimming pool, hydrotherapy rooms, and solariums for heliotherapy, the practice of exposing a patient to ultraviolet lights. (Courtesy of the Pennsylvania State Archives.)

The gymnasium provided room for children to play basketball and volleyball. The gym was surrounded by balconies for spectators to view games. Staff also used this space to teach the children line dancing. (Courtesy of the Pennsylvania State Archives.)

In the 24th annual report, Dr. Klopp reminded the board of trustees that there had been no new construction on the hospital grounds since 1932. As a result, the hospital became increasingly overcrowded and was in desperate need of expansion. In 1937, the General State Authority Board approved a $1,029,000 budget for the expansion of the hospital, and Dr. Klopp immediately got to work. The new budget allowed him to build five new buildings on the hospital grounds, including a convalescent building, a nurses' home, a children's building, a disturbed women's building, and a dining hall. Klopp stated in an interview that these buildings were his greatest accomplishment. (Courtesy of the Pennsylvania State Archives.)

This is the second children's building on the hospital's grounds. Once completed, it would house girls and the previous children's building would be converted to boys only. This new building would include a library, doctor's office, swimming pool, and school rooms. (Courtesy of the Pennsylvania State Archives.)

Upon its completion in 1939, the building would add an additional 72 beds to the hospital campus. Due to a lack of funds for furnishing, it sat vacant until 1941. The total cost for the construction of this single building came to $169,235. (Courtesy of the Pennsylvania State Archives.)

This is the children's building reaching the end of construction. All sleeping quarters for the girls were on the third floor, with classrooms on the second. The addition of the girls' building allowed the hospital to extend the ages admitted. (Courtesy of the Pennsylvania State Archives.)

This photograph, taken in the mid-1940s, shows the girls' building completely finished. Behind it is the previous children's building, which would later be renamed after Dr. Henry Klopp. After these buildings closed down, they were purchased by Community Services for Children Inc. and turned into a youth center. (Courtesy of the Pennsylvania State Archives.)

The convalescent building was a critical part of Dr. Klopp's vision for patients being able to heal and return to society. Dr. Klopp had pushed for the development of a convalescent building since the day he took the position in 1912. (Both, courtesy of the Pennsylvania State Archives.)

On March 21, 1941, the convalescent building was opened and ready for occupancy. This building added 68 beds to the hospital, and 42 patients were transferred to it on opening day. Unlike other wards on the hospital grounds, this building was considered an "open ward," meaning there was freedom to move around as the doors were not locked. Some notable features were a men's barber shop, a hairdressing room, and a manicure room. (Both, courtesy of the Pennsylvania State Archives.)

The disturbed women's building was at the back of the hospital property. It was divided into two units, each holding 40 patients. The first floor included a dining room with a cafeteria, occupational therapy rooms, open air porches, and neutral baths with special temperature controls. Dr. Klopp noted in his reports how he enjoyed watching the transfer of patients to the new buildings and was excited to hear them tell him how much they enjoyed the smaller sleeping arrangements. (Both, courtesy of the Pennsylvania State Archives.)

One major improvement to the hospital that was required was an updated boiler plant. On February 4, 1938, a contract was awarded to Coxe Stoker Engineering Company of Hazelton, Pennsylvania, for $184,698 to install a new boiler plant. This new installation included three 500-horsepower Stoker fired boilers, an inside coal storage bunker and coal conveyor, a new radial brick chimney, piping, blower fans, and more. The complete dismantling and removal of the old boilers was also required. (Both, courtesy of the Pennsylvania State Archives.)

Because of the increase in staff, a new dining hall was also required. The total cost of this structure was $81,164. Once completed, it sat idle for two years due to a lack of funds to furnish it. The photograph above shows the foundation of the building behind the auditorium. The image below shows the final stages of construction. (Both, courtesy of the Pennsylvania State Archives.)

One thing that was common among state hospitals was their elaborate tunnel systems, used for piping and building maintenance. These tunnels connected all the buildings on the hospital grounds and provided a sheltered route for the staff to travel from building to building during harsh weather. Also, if there was a death on the property, the body could be moved to the onsite morgue via the tunnels. (Both, courtesy of the Pennsylvania State Archives.)

The female attendants building was built to give female nurses a place to live on campus. The first floor had full-length windows in the rear and included waiting rooms, a social room, and a kitchenette. Nine bedrooms were on the first floor, 15 on the second, and 15 on the third floor. All the nurses shared one central bathroom and shower room. The total cost of this building came to $79,870. (Both, courtesy of the Pennsylvania State Archives.)

Once completed, this building added a total of 50 rooms for staff housing. In addition to the living rooms, a reception area was added, along with a social room and a kitchen. Staff also were able to sit out on the open-air porch. (Courtesy of the Pennsylvania State Archives.)

This photograph was taken by Janice Painter, who worked and lived in this building. The photograph can be dated around 1945. It was not uncommon to see nurses sitting out on the grass in front of the building or lounging on the porch. (Courtesy of the Painter/Resse family.)

This photograph was taken in the mid-1940s at the female attendants building. Nurses are lounging on the porch after their shifts. Staff were also allowed to use the indoor swimming pools for relaxation. Other areas for patients and staff to enjoy included a bowling alley, baseball fields, and tennis courts. (Courtesy of the Painter/Resse family.)

Upon completion of all these new buildings in 1942, the hospital was viewed as one of the most modern of its time. The total cost of all the buildings was approximately $1.25 million, compared to the original budget of $1,029,000. In 1942, the hospital's population had reached over 1,700 patients. (Courtesy of the Pennsylvania State Archives.)

This is an aerial view of the hospital grounds in 1966. From the time the hospital was built in 1912 to the end of 1942, the hospital had almost doubled in size. (Courtesy of the Pennsylvania State Archives.)

In 1942, Dr. Henry Klopp announced his retirement after being at the hospital for 30 years. He was the longest-serving superintendent at the hospital and is remembered for his dedication to the children. Dr. Klopp spent the majority of his life focusing on changing standards and pioneering improvements to the mental health system. On March 7, 1945, he passed away from heart complications at Hahnemann Hospital in Philadelphia. (Courtesy of the Pennsylvania State Archives.)

Five
TURNOVER AND TREATMENT

Since the opening of Allentown State Hospital, Dr. Harry Hoffman has always been present on the hospital grounds as the assistant superintendent and clinical director. In June 1942, Dr. Hoffman took over as superintendent, with Dr. Klopp staying on for one more year to assist with the transition before retiring to the Hotel Traylor in Allentown. (Courtesy of the Allentown Public Library.)

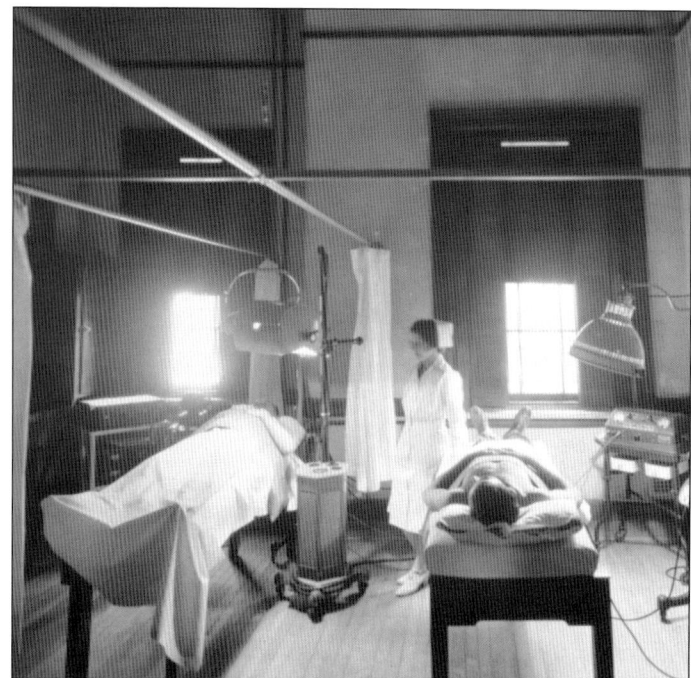

These patients are undergoing heliotherapy, sometimes referred to as phototherapy or sun therapy. This was an ideal treatment for patients suffering from lupus. Patients were given goggles to protect their eyes and then exposed to artificial sources of ultraviolet, visible, or infrared light. This treatment would kill bacteria on the skin. These patients also spent as much time as possible outside exposed to natural sunlight. (Courtesy of the Pennsylvania State Archives.)

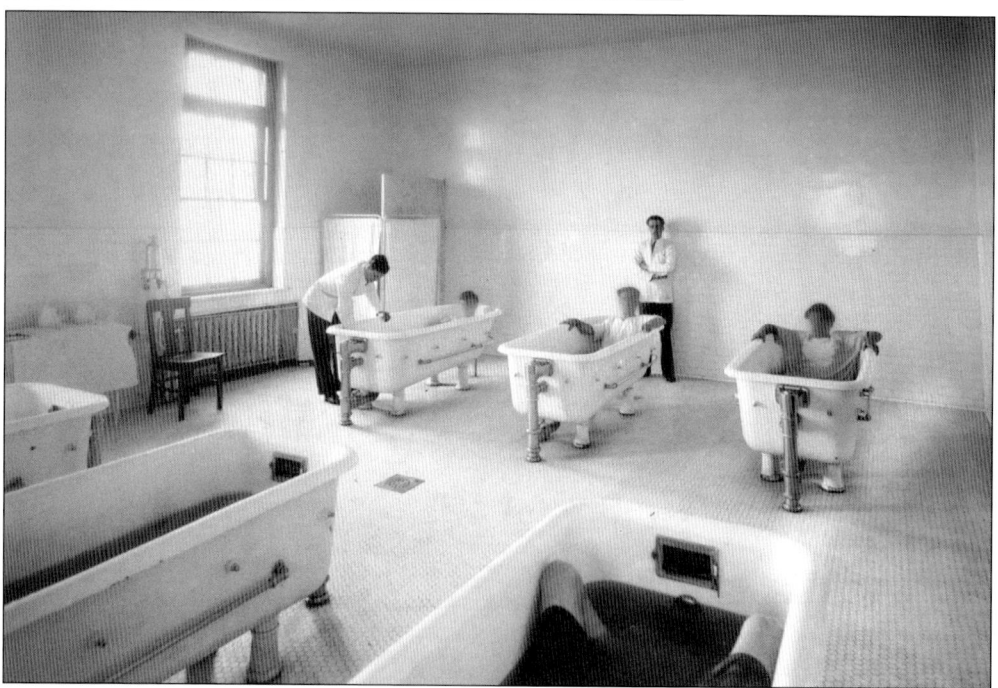

By 1944, Allentown State Hospital had 43 of the tubs seen here and seven hydriatric rooms. This form of treatment, known as hydrotherapy, was the most-recognized treatment of the 20th century. Patients were placed in tubs for extended periods. The temperature was selected based on what staff thought would be the most effective. The water would be cold for those in an aggravated state, and warm for those suffering from anxiety or depression. (Courtesy of the Pennsylvania State Archives.)

Heliotherapy is being performed on boys in the children's unit. Later, the children's unit was renamed the Klopp building after the hospital's first superintendent, Dr. Henry Klopp. (Courtesy of the Pennsylvania State Archives.)

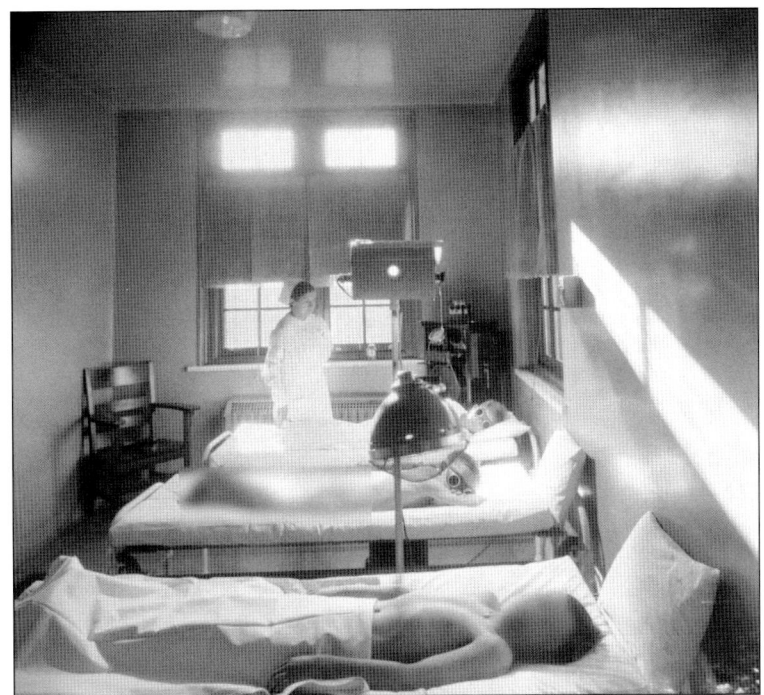

Occupational therapy played an important role at Allentown State Hospital. Many patients enjoyed the opportunity to work around the hospital or on the farm in Weaversville instead of lying in bed or lounging in day rooms. The hospital aimed to be as self-sufficient as possible. Some of the crafts included woodworking, painting, basketry, leatherwork, chip carving, embroidering, sewing, book binding, and Indian beadwork. This photograph shows the occupational therapy room for females. (Courtesy of the Allentown Public Library.)

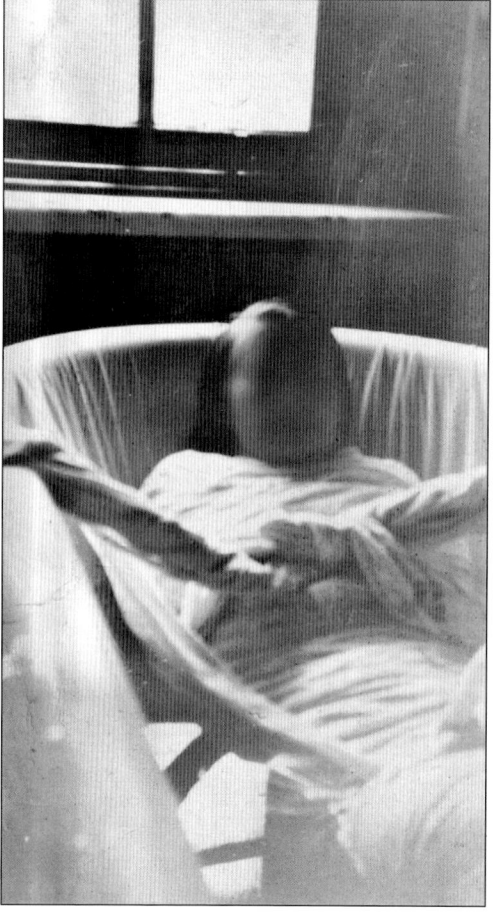

Above is the occupational therapy room for men in 1925. Toys for children can be seen on tables in the back, made by adult patients. Patients also enjoyed book reading clubs, where they would read out loud, which benefited those who could not read or had poor vision. At left is another common form of therapy conducted at the hospital, called a wet wrap or wet sheet pack. This involved a patient being wrapped in wet sheets followed by dry sheets to regulate evaporation and temperature. This technique was used as a way to calm patients or reduce fevers. (Above, courtesy of the Allentown Public Library; left, courtesy of the Painter/Reese family.)

In June 1950, Dr. Harry Hoffman announced his retirement and that Dr. Roy Goshorn (first row, second from left) would replace him. Dr. Goshorn had previously worked at Allentown State Hospital from 1929 to 1934, but left to start a private practice, later becoming superintendent of Hollidaysburg State Hospital in 1937. Dr. Goshorn served as an expert witness in the 1950s Falcone murder trial. (Courtesy of the Pennsylvania State Archives.)

In 1954, a new state secretary of welfare, Harry Shapiro, began putting pressure on state hospitals in an effort to clean up facilities. He targeted Allentown State Hospital and its board of trustees after claiming to have received a confidential report that the hospital was in deplorable condition. Without being presented with any evidence, the board of trustees was given an ultimatum: remove Dr. Goshorn within 24 hours or be removed. Goshorn was reluctantly removed by the board, who claimed that the decision was not a reflection of Goshorn's performance, but was because of pressure from Shapiro. After Goshorn was removed, Dr. John C. Kistler resigned, claiming that Shapiro's actions were unjust and the work of politics. A temporary superintendent, Dr. Hamblen Eaton, was appointed in early 1955 and was replaced by Dr. Howard T. Fiedler. (Courtesy of the Pennsylvania State Archives.)

Shettel Cottage was a children's unit designed to house 45 children from ages 6 to 12. Built in the late 1960s and opened in 1970, the building cost roughly $500,000 to construct and was named after Dr. Raymond Shettel, who started working at Allentown State Hospital in 1947 as a physician. By 1950, Dr. Shettel was promoted to assistant superintendent. In 1959, he took over the children's division and was known to have a great talent for working with youth. Shettel taught neurology at Hahnemann Medical College in Philadelphia, and was also on the faculty at Lafayette College and Lehigh University. (Courtesy of the Pennsylvania State Archives.)

After the death of Dr. Shettel, Dr. John Roop assumed the position of assistant superintendent. Dr. Roop served as clinical director at Warren State Hospital from 1957 to 1967 before he made the transition to Allentown State Hospital. In May 1973, Roop was promoted to superintendent on the retirement of Dr. Fiedler. Roop served as superintendent of Allentown State Hospital until 1984, turning over the position to Dale Newhart. Highly skilled in employee relations, Roop was credited with bringing a team approach to Allentown State Hospital. He also implemented a program that compensated patients for any labor they performed at the hospital. (Courtesy of the Pennsylvania State Archives.)

Above is a staff meeting of the hospital's administration. Dr. Howard T. Fiedler, at bottom left, is conversing with Dr. Raymond Shettel. Dr. Fiedler served as superintendent for 17 years before retiring in 1972. During his time, he was responsible for the construction of Shettel Cottage and the administration building, which would eventually be named the Fiedler administration building. The photograph below was taken from the roof of the new administration building overlooking the maintenance building. (Both, courtesy of the Pennsylvania State Archives.)

In 1963, the federal Mental Retardation Facilities and Community Mental Health Centers Construction Act was passed by Pres. John F. Kennedy, drastically changing the future for state hospitals across the nation. Federal funding was now available to community mental health centers, and there was a push for these facilities to be developed. By the start of the 1980s, 750 community care centers had opened. From 1955 to 1980, the population of state hospitals dropped by 411,000. (Both, courtesy of the Pennsylvania State Archives.)

The photograph above shows the nurses' dormitory. As the hospital continued to shrink in size, there was no need for nurses to live onsite anymore. This building was renamed Ritter and was leased to the Lehigh Valley Children's Center. The photograph below is looking up at the hospital's main building. (Both, courtesy of the Pennsylvania State Archives.)

From the 1960s on, there was a massive push for deinstitutionalization. New antipsychotic drugs such as thorazine were introduced, replacing treatments such as insulin shock therapy. Allentown State Hospital's population consistently declined until the hospital's closure. (Both, courtesy of the Pennsylvania State Archives.)

Both images were taken in the mid-1970s and show the change of the landscape from the creation of the hospital to the present day. Above is a view of the previous administration building taken from the new administration building. The photograph below was taken from building A, looking toward Hannover Avenue. (Both, courtesy of the Pennsylvania State Archives.)

Dale E. Newhart served as superintendent of Allentown State Hospital from 1984 to 1989. Newhart worked at the hospital for 39 years in various positions, such as accounting and business administration. He was known to fight for higher pay for the staff, often arguing that in order to keep talent, one must pay for it. (Courtesy of the Pennsylvania State Archives.)

Six
A New Era

In this photograph from the 1980s, the previous name of the state hospital can be seen exposed. Due to rotting and decay, the hospital's maintenance staff removed a portion of the hospital entrance. The stone with the name "State Homeopathic Hospital" was taken to the State Museum of Pennsylvania. (Courtesy of John McDevitt.)

In the 1980s, new practices started to emerge around the treatment of children. Unlike the previous years, the hospital started integrating children back into a mix of adults. This provided new coping skills and trained children how to socialize better. At left are children playing in the swimming pool of the Klopp building. Below, a staff member is working with a child on school work. (Both, courtesy of the Pennsylvania State Archives.)

These two photographs show the staff engaging with children at the hospital. Most likely, they were taken at Shettel Cottage. Above is a child describing a toy car to a psychiatrist. Below, a counselor plays a game of checkers with a patient. (Both, courtesy of the Pennsylvania State Archives.)

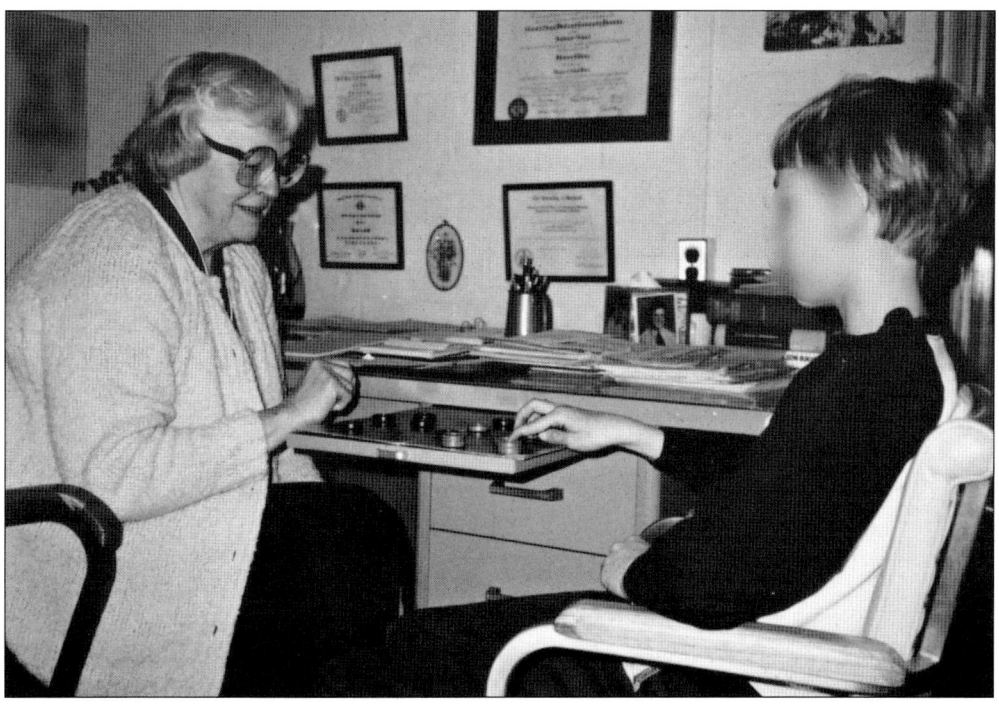

Education played a critical role in the development of patients. Teachers often worked one on one with each student, guiding them through subjects such as math. The above image shows a teacher working with a student. Pictured below is a carnival that was held for patients. (Both, courtesy of the Pennsylvania State Archives.)

Staff and administration tried to provide as many activities as possible for the children of Allentown State Hospital. The photograph below shows a group of children from the hospital enjoying trick or treat in 1983. Above is another fair that the hospital held on its grounds. (Both, courtesy of the Pennsylvania State Archives.)

These two photographs provide two more examples of activities for the children of Allentown State Hospital. At left is an ice-cream truck, and below is a staff member dressed as Smokey the Bear. (Left, courtesy of the Pennsylvania State Archives; below, courtesy of John McDevitt.)

Music therapy was also a big part of the hospital's program for children. Pictured in the late 1980s, staff are singing with the students, who just participated in a baseball game. (Courtesy of the Pennsylvania State Archives.)

These two photographs show students in an art class. The artwork would be put on display for students and staff to see throughout the hospital. Some staff recall the hospital feeling more like a school and less like a hospital. (Both, courtesy of the Pennsylvania State Archives.)

On May 15, 2002, the old employee break room of the main building (above) was completely renovated and turned into a library. Dr. Theodore Millon (below), who served as the president of the board of trustees from 1965 to 1970, donated his entire library to Allentown State Hospital. (Both, courtesy of Gregory Smith.)

Dr. Theodore Millon, seen here cutting the ribbon to the new library, played a pivotal role in turning the hospital around in the mid-1950s by sending the critical report to Shapiro that sparked the termination of Dr. Roy Goshorn. At 26 years old, Dr. Millon served as an assistant professor at Lehigh University. In October 1954, he brought a class to tour Allentown State Hospital, and what he saw compelled him to draft his five-page letter to George M. Leader, a candidate for governor. Harry Shapiro was an aide to Leader and decided to make a surprise visit to the hospital, bringing members of the press. When Leader took office, Shapiro was named secretary of welfare. Within days, Shapiro gave the board of trustees at Allentown State Hospital an ultimatum. When some members left the board along with the superintendent, Dr. Millon was brought in. Within five years, Allentown State Hospital went from being one of the worst to one of the best. Millon was known to dress as a patient and wander the halls of the hospital, sitting and talking with patients to learn as much as he could. (Courtesy of Gregory Smith.)

Seven
PERT AND THE ROAD AHEAD

In 1999, an inspection of the state hospital system was conducted by the Joint Commission on the Accreditation of Healthcare Organizations (JCAHO). Its review revealed that Allentown State Hospital was the first accredited psychiatric hospital in the United States to eliminate the use of seclusion as a procedure in reaction to patients in crisis. Following the JACHO survey, this sign was placed on the hospital's grounds by the main entrance to commemorate this monumental achievement. (Courtesy of Gregory Smith.)

The treatment of those who struggle with mental illness has always been a moral and ethical issue. At the June 27, 1904, cornerstone-laying ceremony for the hospital, Pennsylvania governor Pennypacker (pictured) addressed the crowd, recounting a time when he saw a man shackled with a ball and chain because of his mental illness. Throughout the 20th century to the present, the use of seclusion, mechanical restraints, bed sheets, padded mittens, and chemical restraints was common in psychiatric hospitals, including Allentown State Hospital. These measures were often the first method administered to control a patient in acute psychiatric or behavioral distress. (Courtesy of the Library of Congress.)

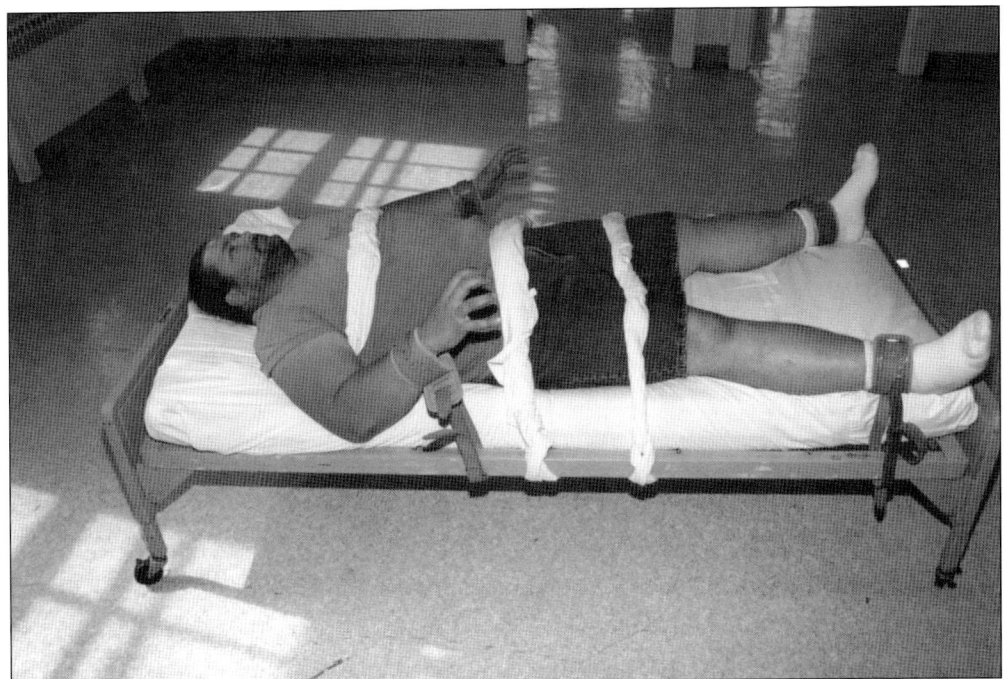

This staff member was placed in a seven point restraint for demonstration purposes. In 1994, a total of 13,427 hours of seclusion and 19,935 hours of mechanical restraint were used. Physical or hands-on restraint and chemical restraint were not yet counted. (Courtesy of Gregory Smith.)

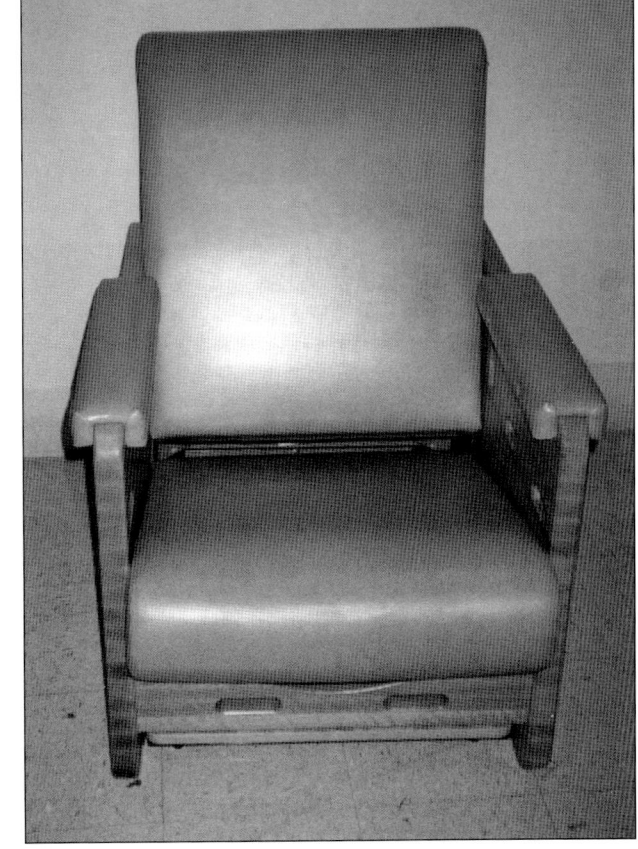

Chairs like this were common in psychiatric facilities and were considered an improvement over the old-style chairs used to restrain patients. They had padding and a low center of gravity to prevent accidental tip overs. These updated chairs featured slots where mechanical restraint devices, leather or soft Velcro, would slide through to secure the patient's arms and legs. (Courtesy of Cynthia Kromer.)

In 1988, senior staff began reviewing data on how the hospital responded to patients in crisis. A typical ward was made up of over 40 patients supported by three direct care workers and a nurse. Teams would be led by a psychiatrist and supported by a social worker, psychologist, occupational therapist, and recreation staff. This resulted in a confusing lack of structure and leadership. Patients in crisis often ended up in restraint and seclusion. It was not uncommon for these procedures to be ordered in anticipation of a patient's future actions. Orders given for containment usually were lengthy, and it was not unusual for a person to be placed in seclusion for eight hours or more. Any training staff received for crisis intervention focused on how to apply a restraint or physical hold. Very little attention was given to verbal de-escalation techniques. (Courtesy of the Pennsylvania State Archives.)

In 1991, leadership began taking steps toward change. A large internal committee was established and tasked with investigating alternative methods for responding to patients in crisis. CEO David Jay (right) and Chief Nurse Executive Richard M O'Dea (below) challenged this group to design a new policy on how to manage psychiatric emergencies within the hospital. Disagreements on how to approach the project quickly surfaced among members, resulting in the committee being reduced to a smaller team. (Right, courtesy of the Jay family; below, courtesy of Theresa O'Dea.)

The team began by researching programs that emphasized a mixture of both verbal de-escalation skills and safe, physical intervention options. The US Department of Veterans Affairs Medical Center in Coatesville, Pennsylvania, met this requirement the best. Its program, called the Psychiatric Emergency Assistance Team (PEAT), emphasized a non-offensive, team response to a psychiatric or behavioral crisis, which addressed the committee's primary safety concerns. The program was modified for use at the hospital, enhancing the verbal de-escalation techniques. (Author's collection.)

Throughout most of 1992, staff continued to train by running mock drills and planning for patients with special needs. In 1993, Allentown State Hospital launched the Psychiatric Emergency Response Team (PERT) as a non-violent, therapeutic approach to supporting patients in psychiatric or behavioral distress. The main focus of PERT was to safely resolve a patient crisis or expected crisis with minimal use of force. A crisis response was considered a success if a containment procedure was not used. Both the staff and patient were safer by talking the patient down rather than using force. (Courtesy of John McDevitt.)

Stater

A Publication of Allentown State Hospital November, 1999

FIRST IN THE NATION!!

For almost as long as I can remember, we have been working diligently on the reduction of the use of seclusion and restraint at ASH. Over the course of the past five years we have moved from one of the highest use facilities in the Commonwealth to one of the lowest. In fact we have become the leading hospital in this area and one that our sister hospitals try to emulate.

In September, I attended a National Summit in Washington D.C. along with the CEO's from all of the hospitals in Pennsylvania and the CEO's from 166 hospitals across the entire United States. During that conference it was announced by Deputy Secretary for Mental Health and Substance Abuse Services, Charles Curie, that Allentown State hospital had totally eliminated the use of seclusion. He went on to report that we have not used seclusion for more than a year. The response from those present was very gratifying. In fact, we are receiving calls on a daily basis from many other states asking for our secret. My response is to tell them; "At ASH we have reeducated ourselves and consciously strive to treat everyone of our patients with dignity and respect at all times. We involve every patient in his or her treatment. We have expanded our program offerings and we have learned to be more tolerant of others. In short, we have found that the more you do with people, the less you have to do to them!"

On November 19, many of you joined me and our patients in the main auditorium to celebrate the first anniversary of the total elimination of seclusion. What a great party it was! How proud you should be of your hard work and of the positive impact you have had on the lives of those we serve. During the celebration, Deputy Secretary Curie presented us with a plaque that will hang in our lobby for all to see. He shared his words of commendation and his personal regards for the excellent work done at ASH.

The road to this achievement has not been easy. Now we lead and show others that it is possible. As our reputation spreads, it will ignite the desire in many others to improve. This desire will lead to more effective interventions for patients in many hospitals all because we set the benchmark!

Each employee in this hospital should take pride in this accomplishment and a personal satisfaction for a job well done. We are a great hospital and we prove it more and more everyday!

By: Richard M. O'Dea
Chief Executive Officer
Acting

At first, PERT was met with some resistance by hospital staff. Senior staff and department heads did not like the idea of relinquishing control over how codes were managed. The PERT planning group listened to the concerns of both patients and staff, and made changes as needed. This approach to modifying the program accounted for its quick success and the positive reception the program received as time went on. (Courtesy of Gregory Smith.)

ALLENTOWN STATE HOSPITAL
1600 HANOVER AVENUE
ALLENTOWN, PENNSYLVANIA 18103-2498

COMMONWEALTH OF PENNSYLVANIA
DEPARTMENT OF PUBLIC WELFARE

March 17, 2000

Dear

Last week our hospital was surveyed by JCAHO in the first ever statewide system survey. The result of the survey is an outstanding success for our hospital. We had only two type 1 recommendations and an overall score of 92. This is the highest score we have ever achieved and is 8 points above the current national average for all hospitals surveyed by JCAHO.

In addition to the excellent score, the surveyors reported their positive observations of a dedicated staff who have a "Patient first" attitude. They were impressed with our many efforts to improve patient care and the administrative survey member of the team summed up their opinion of us when he said, "I would be proud to work here"!

You too should be proud of your efforts and your commitment to improving the service we provide. This milestone in our history was achieved by the hard work of a dedicated staff. This hard work has now been validated by an independent accrediting body and our efforts to "Make ASH Shine" have certainly worked!

On behalf of the entire Executive Staff and the patients we serve, congratulations and thanks for a job well done!

Sincerely,

J. Andrew Burkins
Asst. Supt. for Clinical Services

Charles K. Rosenberry
Asst. Supt. for Administration

Bonnie S. Zuber
Client Representative

John J. Drabouski
Director, Performance Improvement

Richard M. O'Dea
Asst. Supt. for Nursing Services

Richard H. Storm
Asst. Supt. for Social/Rehab. Services

Carol F. Eliashevsky
Personnel Director

Gregory M. Smith
Chief Executive Officer

The PERT approach was relentlessly tested over the next few years. Hospital staff would call out a multitude of different codes to challenge PERT and see how the teams would respond. PERT repeatedly proved to be successful with its non-aggressive techniques and verbal communication with patients who were in crisis. In 1996, JCAHO came to inspect Allentown State Hospital. JCAHO surveyors were presented with data showing a significant decrease in the use of seclusion and restraints. In 1993, the total number of hours patients were put in seclusion was 6244.9. By 1996, that number had significantly dropped to 383.93. The number of hours patients were put in restraints drastically decreased as well, from a high of 19,886.5 hours in 1993 to 2,241.27 hours by 1996. (Courtesy of Cynthia Kromer.)

At any given time, there were about 40 PERT team members led by the PERT steering committee. PERT included staff from every area of the hospital, including nursing, social service, psychology, recreation, occupational therapy, security, and staff development. Nursing staff would supplement those teams when there were not enough volunteers. All staff, including non-team members, were trained in the PERT approach and its function. Actual PERT team members were not compensated or paid more for being a PERT team member. They were an all-volunteer group of first responders. A first- or second-shift PERT team typically consisted of seven staff and a captain who was an experienced PERT team member chosen for their leadership skills and commitment to a safe and therapeutic crisis response. PERT team members would carry pagers and respond to any call on the days they were assigned. By 1999, a psychiatrist and/or medical doctor were made a formal part of the daily PERT response team. Pictured here are PERT team members at the 20th anniversary of PERT. (Courtesy of Gregory Smith.)

A typical PERT response would begin with staff calling extension No. 6300, connecting them to the hospital public address system. The caller would announce "code orange" and the location of the emergency. Assigned team members that day would stop what they were doing and report to the location of the crisis. If the patient was physically assaulting an individual or engaged in self-injurious behavior, the team would respond and try to separate the people involved. Once the altercation was stopped, the PERT team members would go about calming the scene by turning off TVs and radios, escorting other patients away, removing any object that could be used to cause harm, and attempting to engage the individual in crisis by using therapeutic dialog. Only one person communicated with the person in crisis and that was usually, but not always, the PERT captain. The time to accomplish this was not limited. After the PERT call was concluded, the patient and staff would go through a debriefing session to help identify what happened and how similar situations could be avoided in the future. The pin pictured here was given to PERT team members.

Between 1993 and 2000, the implementation of PERT led to a significant decrease in the use of seclusion and restraint and injuries attributed to patient-to-patient and patient-to-staff assaults. Additionally, by 1999, this interdisciplinary response team process enabled the hospital to discontinue the use of seclusion as a procedure in reaction to a patient crisis. By the end of 1999, the last of the 23 seclusion rooms at the hospital were converted to multipurpose rooms, patient activity areas, and private rooms. This photograph shows a staff member reenacting a patient in seclusion. (Courtesy of Gregory Smith.)

Allentown State Hospital's work gained national attention in October 2000, when the Pennsylvania Office of Mental Health and Substance Abuse Services won an Innovations in American Government award. The state hospital system competed against more than 1,600 applicants nationwide. The state also received a $100,000 grant from Harvard University's John F. Kennedy School of Government, with funding from the Ford Foundation, to study the effects and implications of this change. (Courtesy of Gregory Smith.)

Gregory M. Smith joined Allentown State Hospital as its chief executive officer in 1997. He came to the hospital with more than 20 years of experience in healthcare leadership. Passionate about the humane and moral treatment of the mentally ill, Smith quickly connected with the PERT approach and became involved, working alongside Richard O'Dea and the rest of the PERT members. Smith collected data on the use of mechanical restraints and seclusion in each of Pennsylvania's remaining state hospitals covering the years 1990 to 2001. Smith's data presented a clear picture of the effect PERT had on reducing and eliminating the use of containment procedures. Between 2001 and 2009, ASH welcomed clinicians from around the world who wanted to see firsthand the work of the PERT teams and learn from the hospital's success. ASH staff also coached hospitals in Europe and other states on how to start a PERT team. Many mental health systems around the world have adopted the PERT approach based on the Allentown model. (Courtesy of Gregory Smith.)

In 2006, Toon van Meel (left), a nurse and manager at the mental health organization Emergis in the Netherlands, came to Allentown State Hospital along with 12 other psychologists and psychiatrists to study the PERT program. Upon his return home, he began applying the skills learned at Allentown at his own hospital. As a result of instituting the PERT approach, Emergis was able to reduce the use of containment procedures by 75 percent in the first year. In 2008, van Meel was awarded the Johannes van Duuren award by the Netherlands national Ministry for Mental Health for his efforts and leadership in reducing seclusion and restraints at Emergis. Though proud to receive the award, van Meel felt it truly belonged to Gregory Smith and the staff at Allentown State Hospital. In 2013, Smith and van Meel reconnected at the eighth European Congress on Violence in Clinical Psychiatry in Ghent, Belgium. After five years, van Meel was finally able to turn over the Johannes van Duuren prize to Smith. (Courtesy of Gregory Smith.)

In 2019, the PERT approach, based on the Allentown model, was officially recognized by The World Health Organization as a sanctioned method for supporting people in psychiatric or behavioral crisis by making it part of its QualityRights Initiative and training guide for mental health care worldwide. Mental health organizations across the world are now introducing the strategies of PERT into their own programs, including law enforcement. (Courtesy of Wikimedia Commons.)

Since Gregory Smith's departure from Allentown State Hospital in 2009, he has continued to be an avid supporter and teacher of PERT's methods. In 2015, Smith became an adviser and contributor to the World Health Organization on mental health recovery, specializing in non-offensive techniques in supporting people in crisis. He continues to lecture and promote these techniques across the globe. (Courtesy of Elizabeth Smith.)

Eight
FIGHTING FOR TOMORROW

On October 7, 2009, a state welfare official made a statement that strongly hinted at the possibility of closing Allentown State Hospital, which triggered an outcry from area lawmakers, residents, and staff. Since 1979, the state had closed 12 of its psychiatric hospitals in an attempt to reduce spending and move toward more of a community-care model. At the time of the announcement, there were 170 patients and 389 employees at ASH. (Courtesy of Gregory Smith.)

In November 2009, a group of workers along with a bipartisan group of elected officials protested the news of the closure in front of the hospital entrance. They were concerned that removing patients from an environment they were used to and having them start over in a new facility would be traumatizing and detrimental to their health. For those who would be transferred to another state hospital, the options were Clarks Summit in Lackawanna County or Wernersville in Berks County, both about an hour away from their families in the Lehigh Valley. (Both, courtesy of Robert Lewis)

From October to December 2009, no official confirmation came from Harrisburg on whether the hospital was to remain or open or closed. However, Allentown State Hospital was tasked with cutting its patient population by one third through the Community-Hospital Integration Project Programs. This program, established in the early 1990s, was designed to help link community programs with the state hospitals in order to help transfer patients ready to be reintegrated into the community. On January 28, 2010, acting public welfare secretary Harriet Dichter announced that Allentown State Hospital would close by the end of 2010. State officials released a statement that they would try to find jobs for the staff, and that 65 of the 174 residents would be transferred to Wernersville State Hospital by July 2010. Surrounding counties were pressured with a 10 month deadline to create individual discharge plans covering living situations and care for the remaining residents. (Courtesy of Gregory Smith.)

With the official announcement of the closure of Allentown State Hospital came a wave of backlash from those in the local community and the medical profession. Hospital staff and family members of patients wrote to local newspapers, concerned that their loved ones would lose the quality of care provided at Allentown State Hospital. A day-long public hearing on the closure was conducted on February 22, 2010, and witnesses were allowed to speak. Gregory M. Smith, former CEO of the hospital, deemed the plan "unsafe" and mentioned some suicides that occurred after Harrisburg State Hospital had closed its doors. David W.P. Jones, coordinator of Allentown State Hospital's closure, denied any relation of suicides to the closure of Harrisburg State Hospital. Former patients praised the care they received at Allentown State Hospital, and feared some current patients would not succeed or end up in jail if outpatient programs were not improved in the Lehigh Valley. (Courtesy of Gregory Smith.)

By August 2010, there were 68 patients in need of a new home and 85 staff members in need of a new job. The Department of Public Welfare worked with surrounding counties to develop residential facilities. Depending on the level of care needed, patients who were reintroduced into the community were placed in a mix of apartments and group homes. For the first year, $109,000 was allocated for each patient's housing and treatment. December 16, 2010, marked the closure of Allentown State Hospital as the last lock was turned by Sherry Snyder, acting deputy secretary of the Office of Mental Health and Substance Abuse Services at the state Department of Public Welfare. Of the 379 employees, 252 were placed into new jobs in various state agencies including the Department of Transportation and Department of Health and Corrections. The patient population was split up, with 125 placed into the community and 60 transferred to Wernersville State Hospital. (Courtesy of Gregory Smith.)

Under Gov. Ed Rendell's administration, Allentown State Hospital was the third state hospital to close in Pennsylvania following Harrisburg in 2006 and Mayview in 2008. The roughly 12-month plan to close ASH was considered aggressive. When Mayview closed its doors, the entire process took 17 months and roughly 17 of the remaining patients were transferred to another state hospital. Patients continued to live at ASH after the closure until their discharge plan was ready. (Courtesy of Gregory Smith.)

In 1946, there were 22 state hospitals in Pennsylvania and six state prisons. As of 2020, there are six remaining state hospitals and the number of correctional facilities has risen to 24. Mental Health America ranks states based on prevalence of mental illness and rate of access to care. In 2019, Pennsylvania ranked 14th in the country. (Courtesy of Gregory Smith.)

With Allentown State Hospital closed, residents of East Allentown and Rittersville would be directly affected by any redevelopment of the hospital grounds. On January 29, 2011, The East Allentown Rittersville Neighborhood Association (EARN) released a statement with a list of key points based on the communities' opinion on redevelopment. EARN requested that the quality of life for the surrounding residents be taken into account and objected to construction of apartments or multifamily housing. If the population of the area was to significantly rise, EARN feared the roads or schools could not handle the influx of residents. (Courtesy of Gregory Smith)

EARN was also concerned about the preservation of historic structures. The tree-lined entrance, main building, and water tower were all requested to be preserved from demolition. If all buildings were to remain intact, EARN was open to the idea of the property being used for a Veterans Affairs hospital, an additional school for the Allentown School District, a private school, or a medical/pharmacy school. In the event that demolition did occur, EARN suggested most of the land remain undeveloped for wildlife and some be converted into athletic fields for residents and youth organizations. Any future buildings that would be developed on the land should remain in the footprint of existing structures. (Courtesy of Gregory Smith.)

In July 2013, Allentown State Hospital was put on the market. This photograph shows a few of the remaining original farm buildings on the grounds. In the distance is Martin Tower, which was demolished in 2019. On November 30, 2018, the Pennsylvania Department of General Services announced demolition plans for the 28 buildings on the ASH campus. Since its closure, the facility has cost approximately $2.2 million a year to maintain, and demolition would cost approximately an additional $15 million. A direct sale of the site to TCA Properties was approved in 2017. On January 15, 2019, local developer and formal mayoral candidate Nat Hyman offered to purchase the property and match the price of the TCA Properties deal with the promise to preserve the buildings. Hyman's deal was rejected, and he would later sue the Department of General Services in an attempt to stop demolition. (Courtesy of Gregory Smith.)

In 2019, Brooke Kemler, a graduate of DeSales University, started an online petition in an attempt to change the state's plans to demolish the hospital structures. Her petition climbed to over 1,000 signatures in the first week. Packets were mailed to state officials with copies of the signatures, examples of alternatives to demolition, and other supporting evidence showing the possibilities of reusing the buildings. Local residents were encouraged to do the same and reach out to their state representatives, voicing their opinions on the closure of the hospital. Kemler was not the only one fighting to stop demolition. Other groups formed to organize protests outside the campus's main entrance. The Allentown City Council also explored options on how to save the historic structure. This photograph is of a public awareness event conducted by Kemler at a showing of the movie *Glass* to raise public awareness and encourage involvement. (Courtesy of Libby Ortiz.)

Sen. Pat Browne of Lehigh introduced a bill in the state legislature on June 3, 2019, directing the Department of General Services to demolish all buildings on the hospital grounds except for an air monitoring station. After all buildings were demolished, the property would be put up for bids and a developer would be chosen based on the best value. On June 11, the Pennsylvania Senate voted 49-0 in favor of Senator Browne's bill. Later, members of the General Assembly voted 200-1 in favor of the bill, sending it to Gov. Tom Wolf, who signed it into effect, securing demolition of the historic structures. This photograph was taken from the hospital grounds looking toward the Lehigh Valley Airport. (Author's collection)

This Photograph was taken on February 23, 2005, from the roof of the administration building by CEO Gregory Smith after the nearly 100-year-old pole lights were replaced so the building could be properly displayed at night. (Courtesy of Gregory Smith.)

Discover Thousands of Local History Books
Featuring Millions of Vintage Images

Arcadia Publishing, the leading local history publisher in the United States, is committed to making history accessible and meaningful through publishing books that celebrate and preserve the heritage of America's people and places.

Find more books like this at
www.arcadiapublishing.com

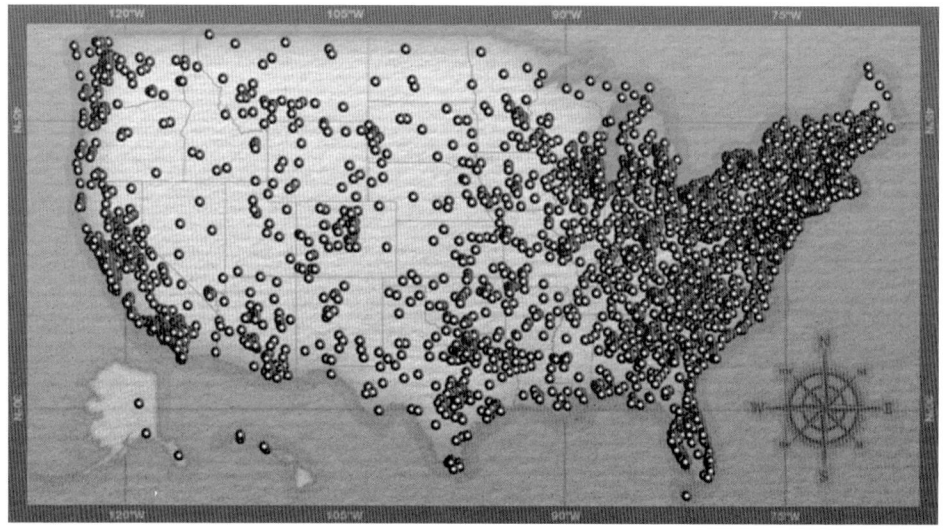

Search for your hometown history, your old stomping grounds, and even your favorite sports team.

Consistent with our mission to preserve history on a local level, this book was printed in South Carolina on American-made paper and manufactured entirely in the United States. Products carrying the accredited Forest Stewardship Council (FSC) label are printed on 100 percent FSC-certified paper.